Zen Doodle Scribbling

Inventing Doodles like Never Before

By Sarah Niland

Table of contents

Disclaimer

While all attempts have been made to verify the information provided in this book, the author does assume any responsibility for errors, omissions, or contrary interpretations of the subject matter contained within. The information provided in this book is for educational and entertainment purposes only. The reader is responsible for his or her own actions and the author does not accept any responsibilities for any liabilities or damages, real or perceived, resulting from the use of this information.

The trademarks that are used are without any consent, and the publication of the trademark is without permission or backing by the trademark owner. All trademarks and brands within this book are for clarifying purposes only and are the owned by the owners themselves, not affiliated with this document.

Introduction

We often doodle, without even realizing that we are creating some forms on the backside of our notebook. More often than not, people often get embarrassed if they are caught doodling. To the surprise of many, these unintentional scribbles that you leave behind on paper margins, notepads, walls, or desktops have significant meaning. Many psychologists around the world have dedicated their lives to the research of doodling. Doodles can even be used to diagnose the emotional issues of people.

The symbols and shapes that you draw reveal a lot about your state of psyche. Even the most innocent and unintentional doodles can carry important messages from your subconscious mind. For instance, people often draw tree when they doodle, and a tree represents life and growth. If you draw a full-grown tree with loads of leaves, it suggests that you are vital and energetic, and you have a strong desire to live. On the other hand, if you draw a leafless tree with weak branches, which is often drawn by the elderly people, it represents a waning will to survive.

Regarding interpretation of symbols, Carl Jung and Sigmund Freud, the pioneers of interpreting symbols, have studied a lot about the subconscious mind.

When you doodle, it becomes a type of free visual association and a method of tapping the reservoirs of deep self- knowledge that is contained in pictures rather than images. However, there are claims that the doodles of an artist mean completely different to him/ her than they do to the psychologist. To this claim, the researchers say that the inferences from the doodles can be drawn only after a careful study of an artist's doodles over several years.

Many symbols represent different meanings. You will read about such symbols and their meanings in the first chapter of this book. If you have read the previous version of this book, you will recognize many things in the Chapter 3 of this book. Nevertheless, this book is also a complete version in itself. You will not find the need to pick up the previous book and flip through its pages. Just go on reading chapter by chapter and you will get the gist of doodling on your own.

Chapter 1

What your Doodles signify

Doodles say a lot about the personality and state of mind of a person, even if he/she is not an artist. When you are stuck somewhere and you incidentally have a pen or pencil in the hand, you might begin doodling anywhere you can. Now, whatever you choose to draw reveals almost everything about your mood and personality. Since people doodle only when they are bored, they are only partially conscious about what they are drawing. It implies that their inner preoccupations come out on the paper.

Some of the common symbols of doodles are stars, boxes, arrows, and flowers. These are the common symbols of feelings and aspirations. If you want to find out the true meaning of a doodle, you must look at the way it is drawn. Emotional people often desire harmony and yearn for affection; they tend to make use of curved lines and rounded shapes. People who are practical or down to earth tend to make use of squares and straight lines. If you are a determined person, you might use zigzags, triangles, and corners. If you are hesitant towards other people, you might use sketchy, light strokes. Similarly, a large size of a doodle represents the outgoing and confident personality of a person. A smaller doodle suggests that a person likes to observe more willingly than participate.

Face

• If a face is well drawn, it means that the artist looks for positive attributes in others. If the face is drawn ugly or weird, it represents the mistrustful attitude of the doodler.

• The expression on the face represents the character or mood of the doodler.

• Comic expression of the face represents the doodler's wish to grab the attention of people. Childish doodles indicate neediness. Profile of the face suggests introvert nature of the artist.

Chessboard

Black and white boxes of the chessboard suggest persistence and patience of the doodler. You might be weighing the options of a tricky situation if you doodle a chequerboard. People who undergo mood swings also draw chessboard.

Flowers

Rounded soft petals around a spherical center of a flower suggest a family centric and amiable person. In case you draw a circular center, but the petals are sharp, you might have a soft heart hiding behind a thorny defensiveness. Lively looking flowers suggest the sociable nature of the artist. If the flower heads are drooping, it represents the burden or worry of the doodler.

Butterflies, bees, and birds

Fluttering butterflies, bees, and birds suggest your romantic and flighty nature. You do not want to be strapped with the problems or tasks of life.

Hearts

A heart is definitely a romantic doodle and it suggests that you love someone.

Intricate Patterns

If you draw highly detailed busy doodles, you have an obsessive nature and you would never allow letting go your loved ones or ambitions. Extreme introverts often draw these patterns.

Ladder or Stairs

These are the symbols of willingness and ambition to have your way of climbing up the staircase of progress. It also suggests that you have a long term and crucial task in hand. They also suggest a spiritual expedition and the desire to have more relaxation and happiness in life.

Arrows

The artist who draws arrows has a certain aim in mind. If he draws an angular or sharp arrow, his target is something important. If the arrow is drawn decorated and more fluid, it suggests a love affair.

Planes and Boats

If you doodle any kind of transportation, it means that you want to escape from something.

House

A house in doodles suggests the want for security. If the house is drawn neat, it indicates a secure life at home. If the house is drawn messy or without windows, it suggests that, the artist is unhappy at home. If the house is drawn on a hilltop, it suggests loneliness of the artist.

Spider's Web

A spider's web indicates a sense of being fenced in or the wish to entice a person into a relationship.

Initials or Names

People who doodle their initials or names often crave for attention. This is particularly common in teenagers. If you doodle the name of another person, it indicates that you are thinking about him/ her or you have a love affair with him/ her. It may also indicate that the other person has preoccupied your mind because they are a reason of some problem for you.

Stars

Ambitious people often draw stars. Several stars in one doodle indicate optimism and a one big, embellished, bold star; you have a certain aim in your life. If you draw a uniform and neat star, it indicates your mental focus. If you draw asymmetric star, you have an energetic personality.

Chapter 2
Patterns of Zen Doodle

In this chapter, you will learn how to create your own doodles. You just need a basic square box and a little bit of creativity to start doodling. Let us begin.

Pattern 1
Benif

Step 1

Draw a square box on a sheet of paper. Divide it into six vertical sections.

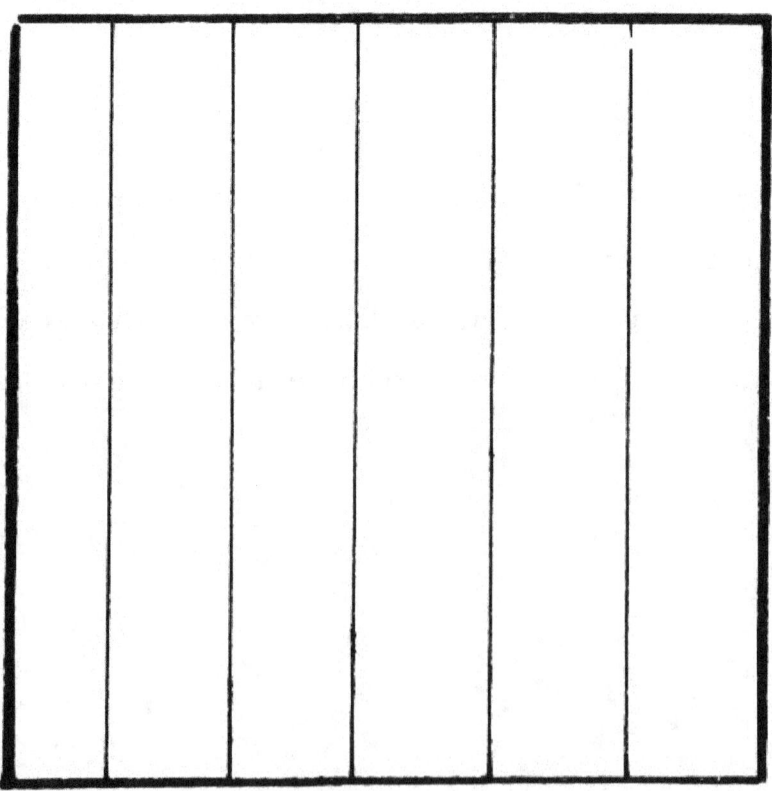

Step 2

Draw a few diagonal lines in the last vertical section as shown in the picture.

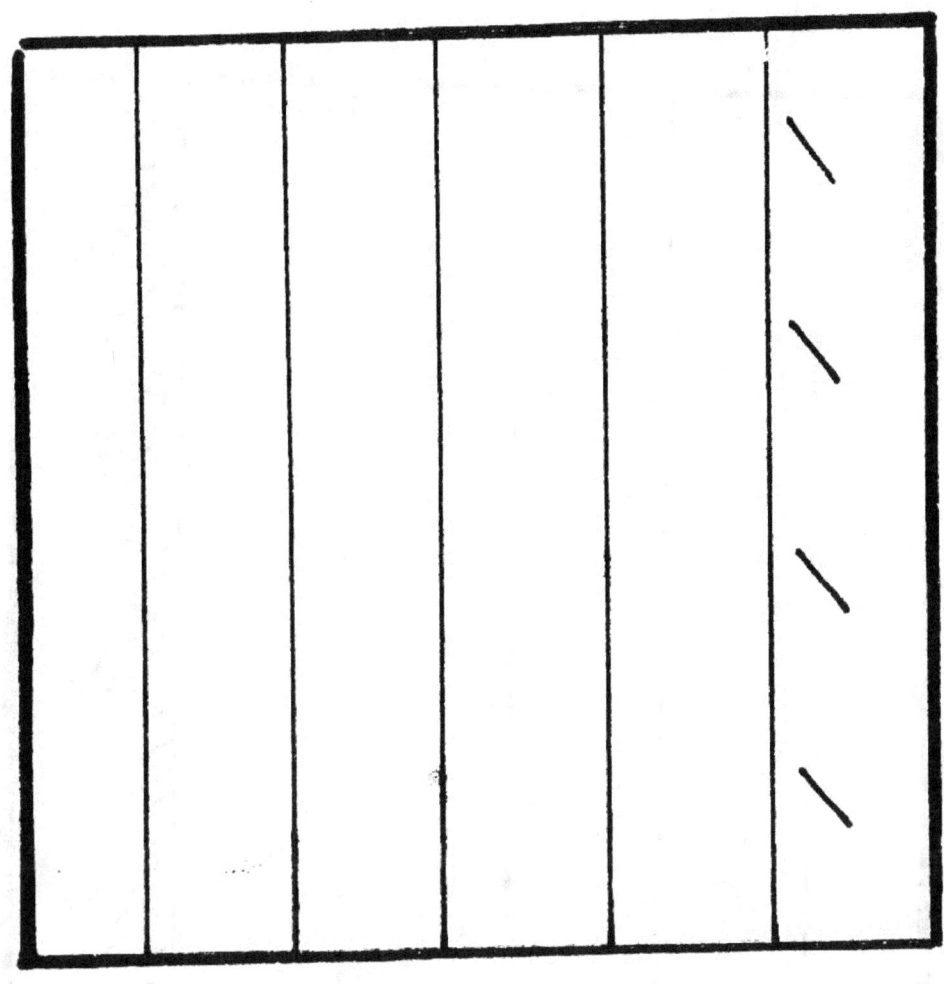

Step 3

Draw a few more diagonal lines with the earlier ones. Draw a few flowers with three petals between the lines as shown in the illustration.

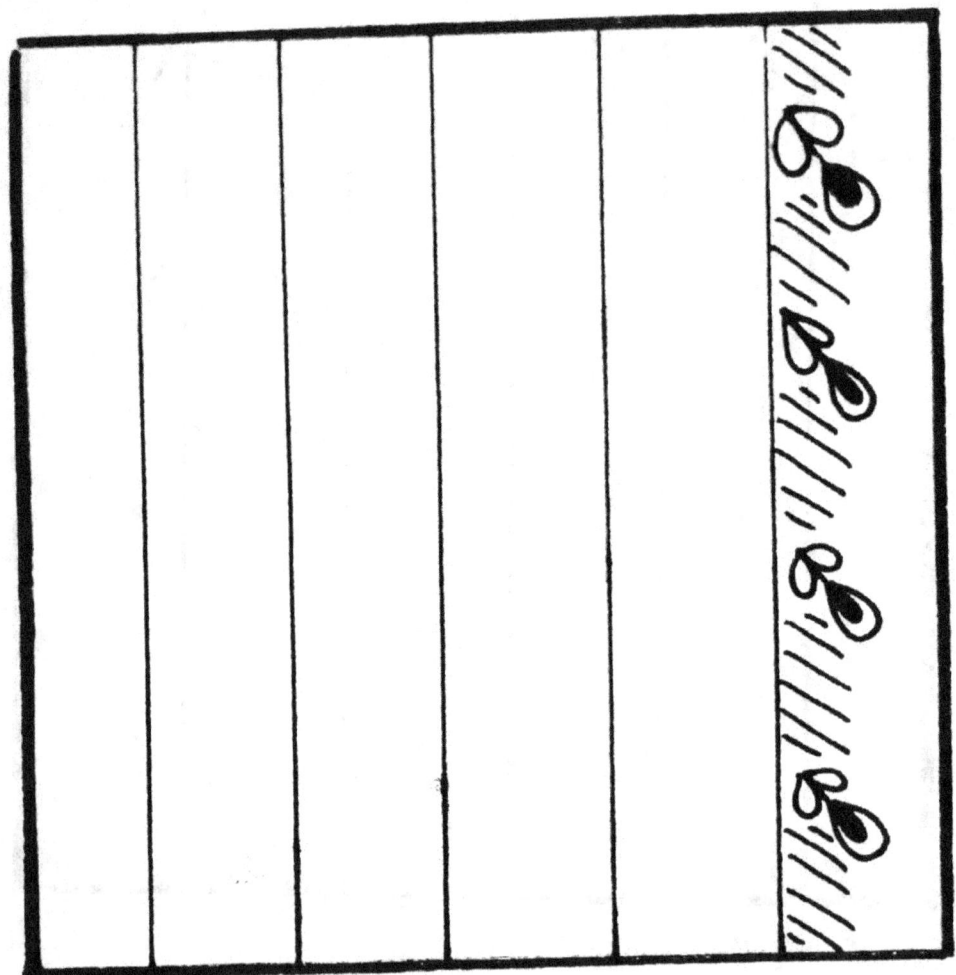

Step 4

Repeat the pattern drawn in the last section for the remaining sections.

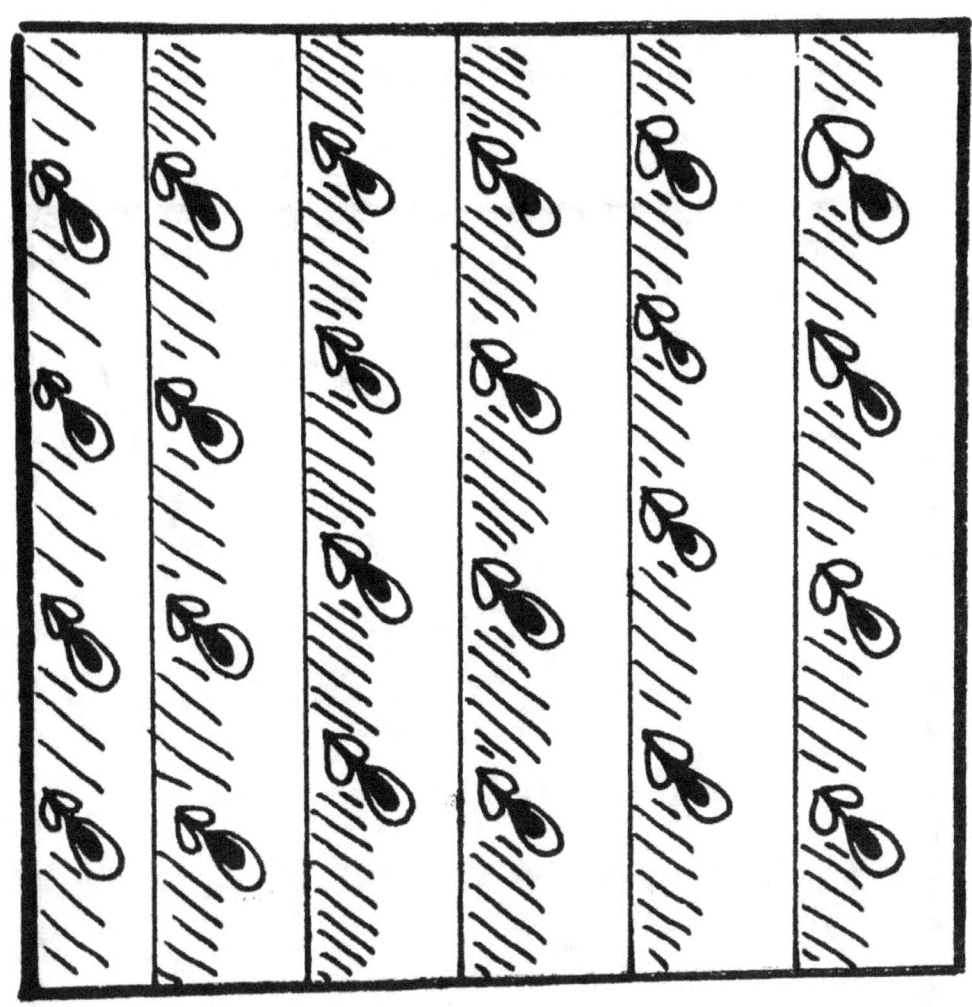

Pattern 2
Flub

Step 1

Draw a square on a sheet of paper.

Draw two V-shapes emerging from any two corners of the box.

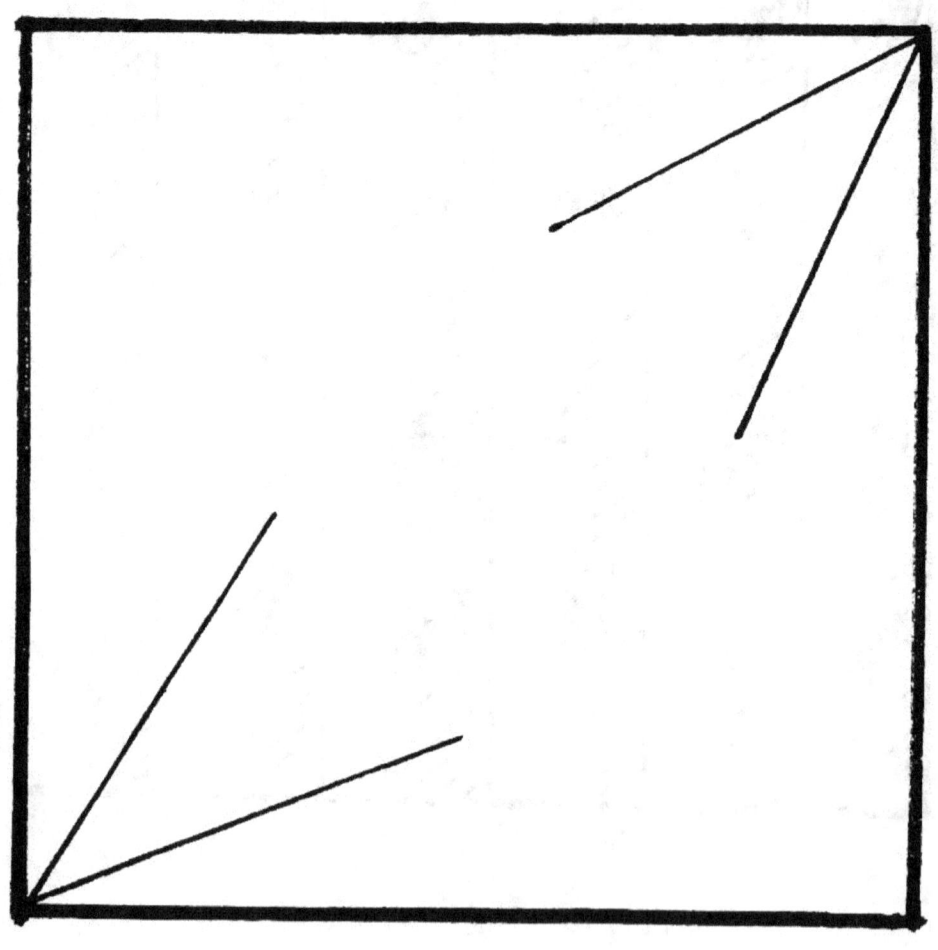

Step 2

From the lower left corner of the box, draw scallops using the V-shape. Draw two circles on the tip of the two arms of V- shape.

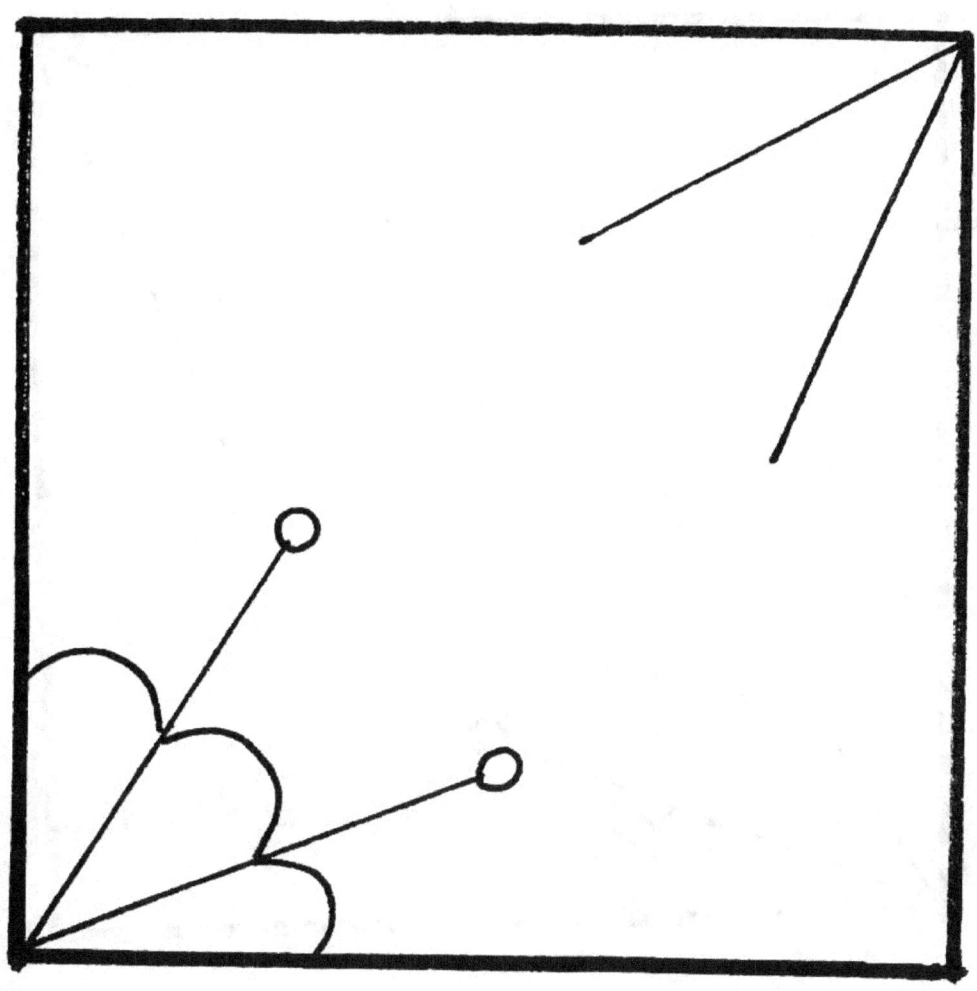

Step 3

Draw a few flower petals on the edge of scallops as shown below.

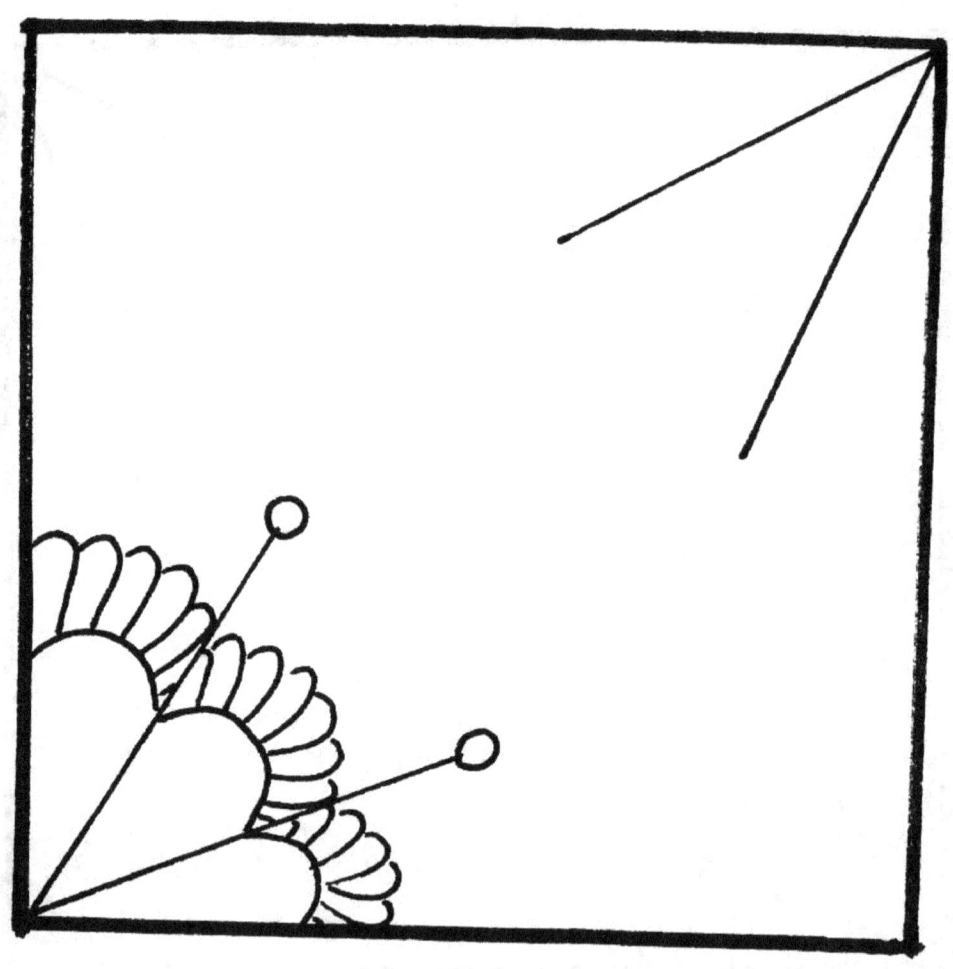

Step 4

Draw a few small circles above the flower petals drawn in the previous step.

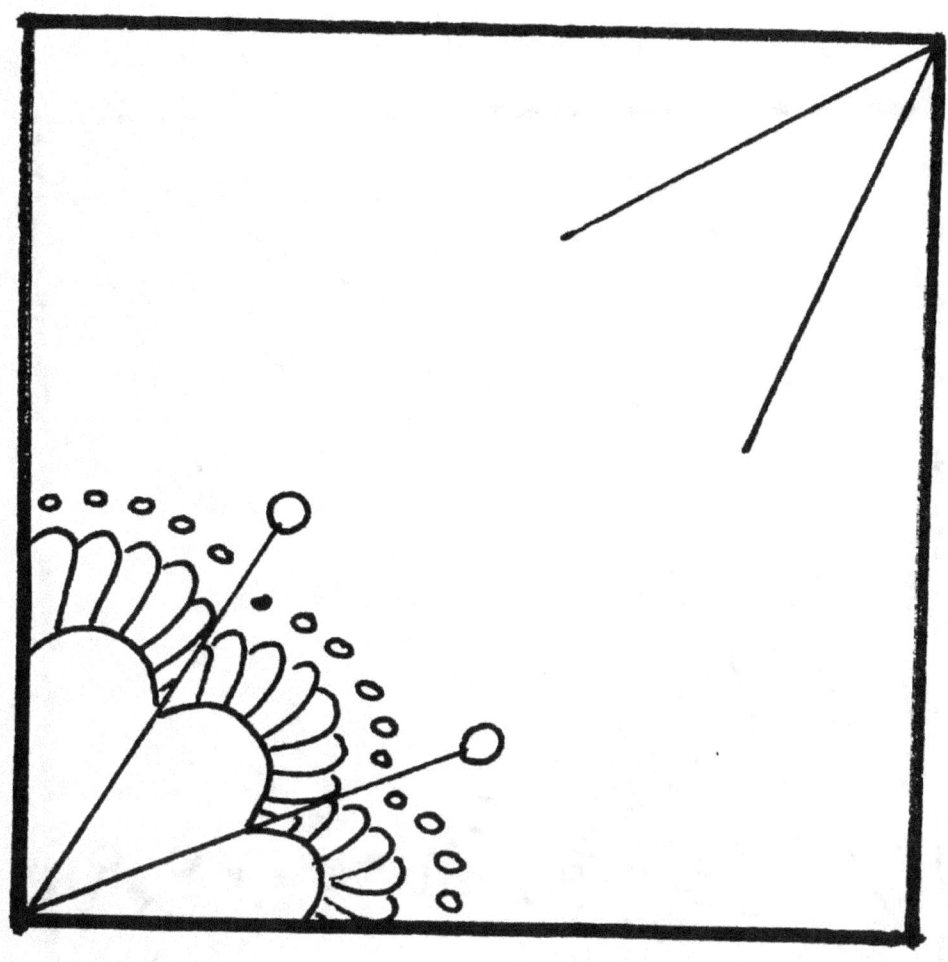

Step 5

Draw three straight lines from the lower right corner of the box and draw small circles on their tips.

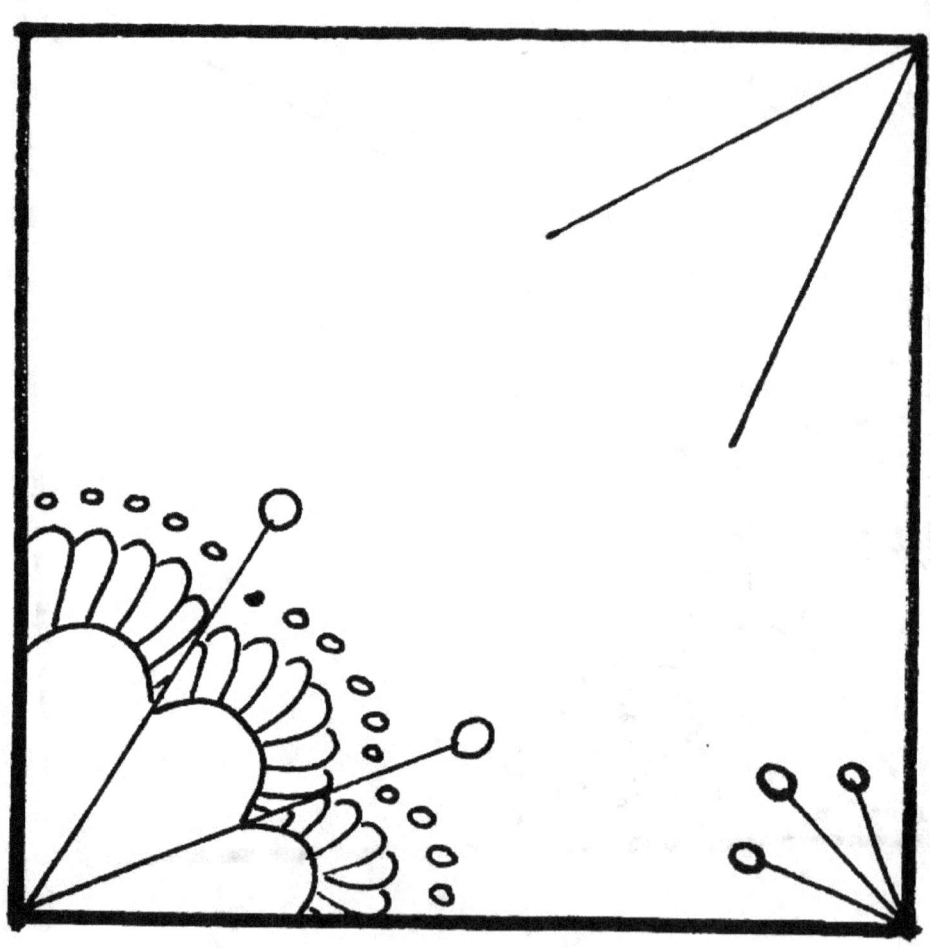

Step 6

Repeat the previous steps for the remaining corners of the box.

The flub pattern is complete.

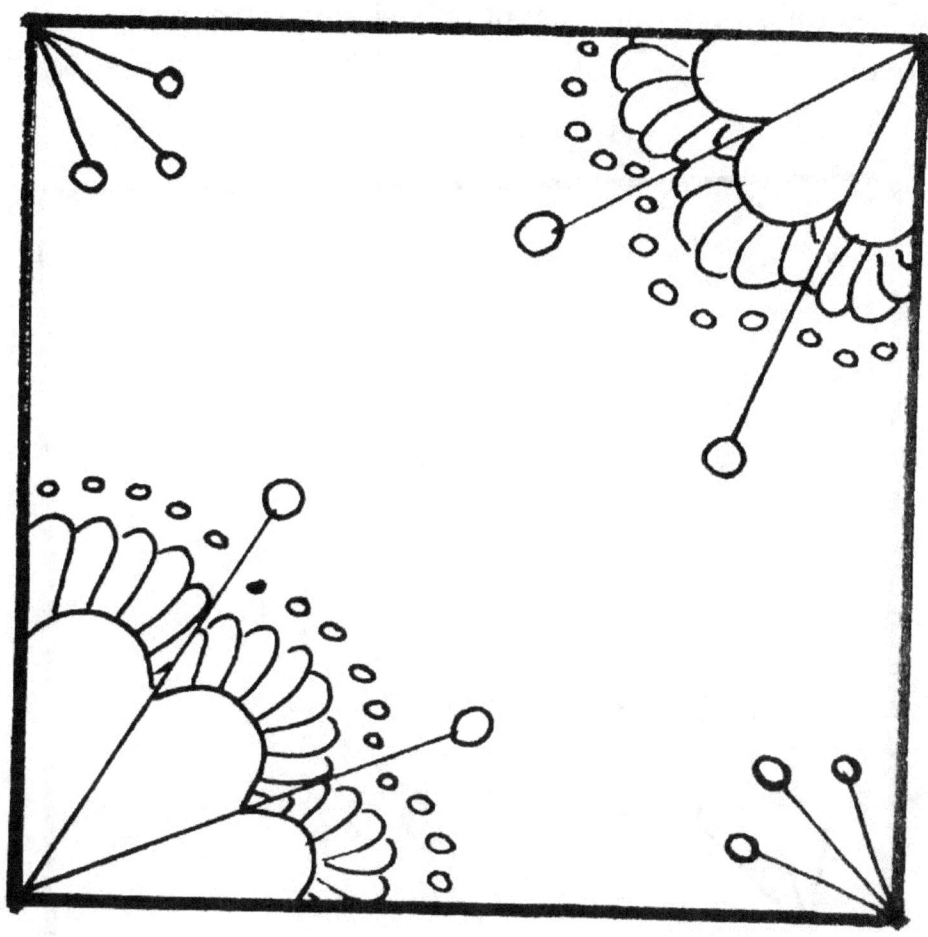

Pattern 3
Galem

Step 1

Draw a square on a sheet of paper.

Draw a few straight lines like that of the twigs of a tree from the lower left corner of the box.

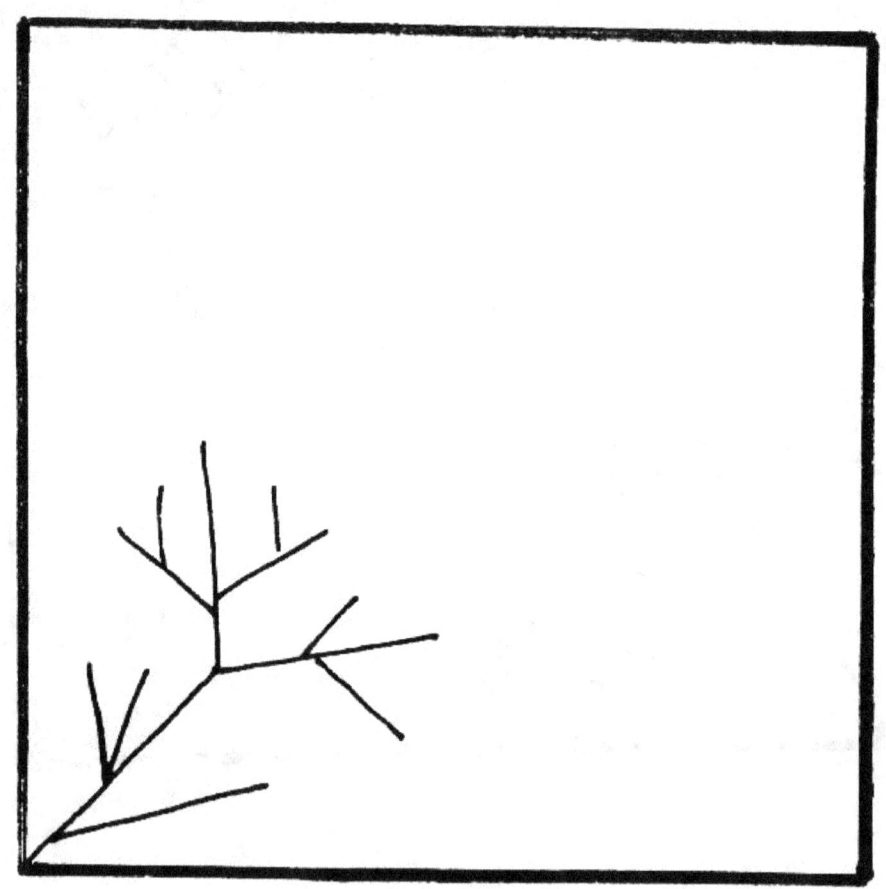

Step 2

Draw similar twig like similar patterns in the remaining corners of the box.

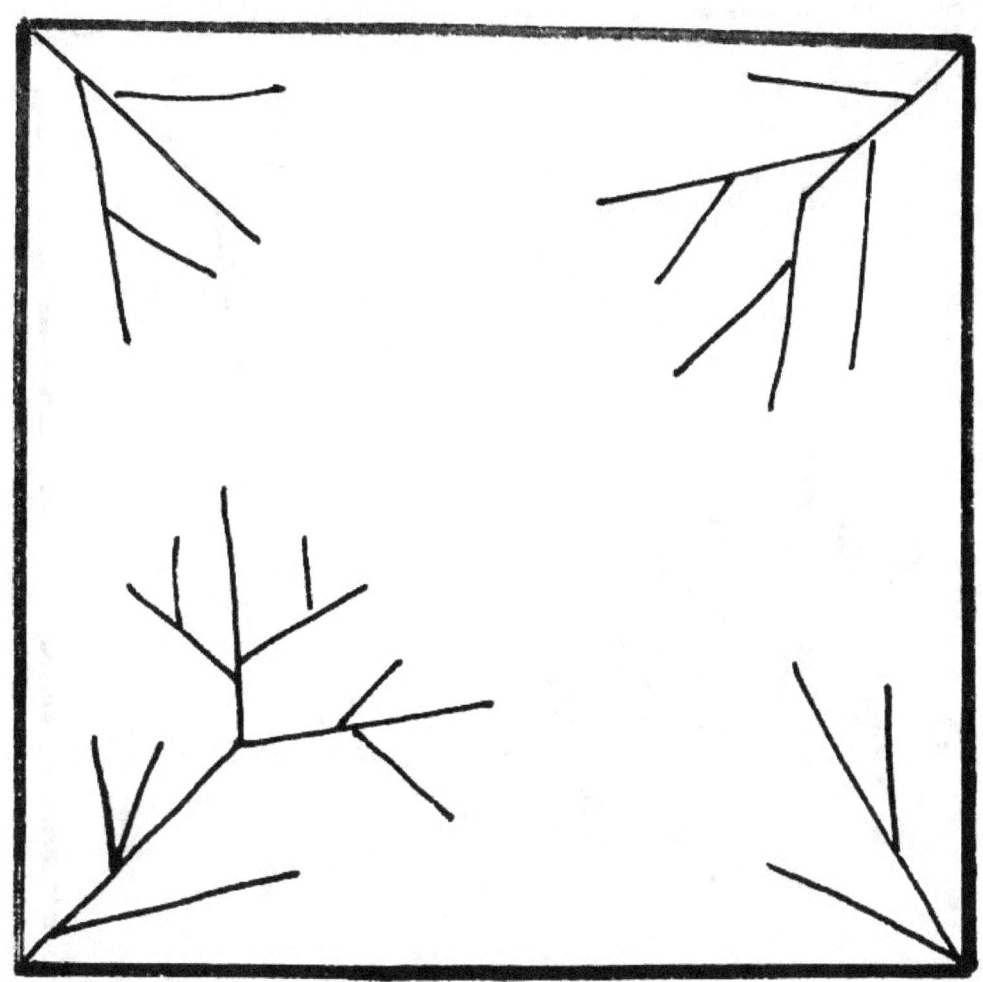

Step 3

On the tip of each twig, draw a drop like shape and fill it with ink.

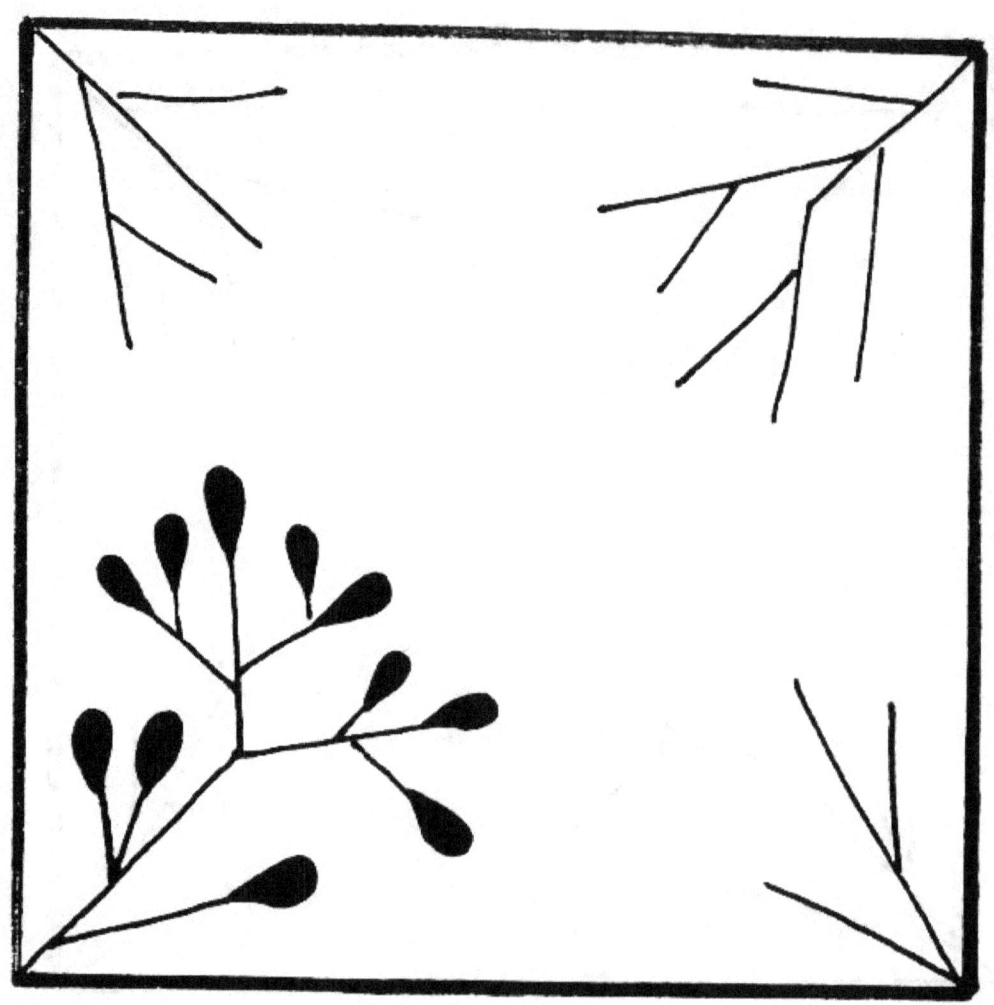

Step 4

Draw similar drop shape on the tip of each tip.

Envelope each drop shape with an outline at some space.

The galem pattern is complete.

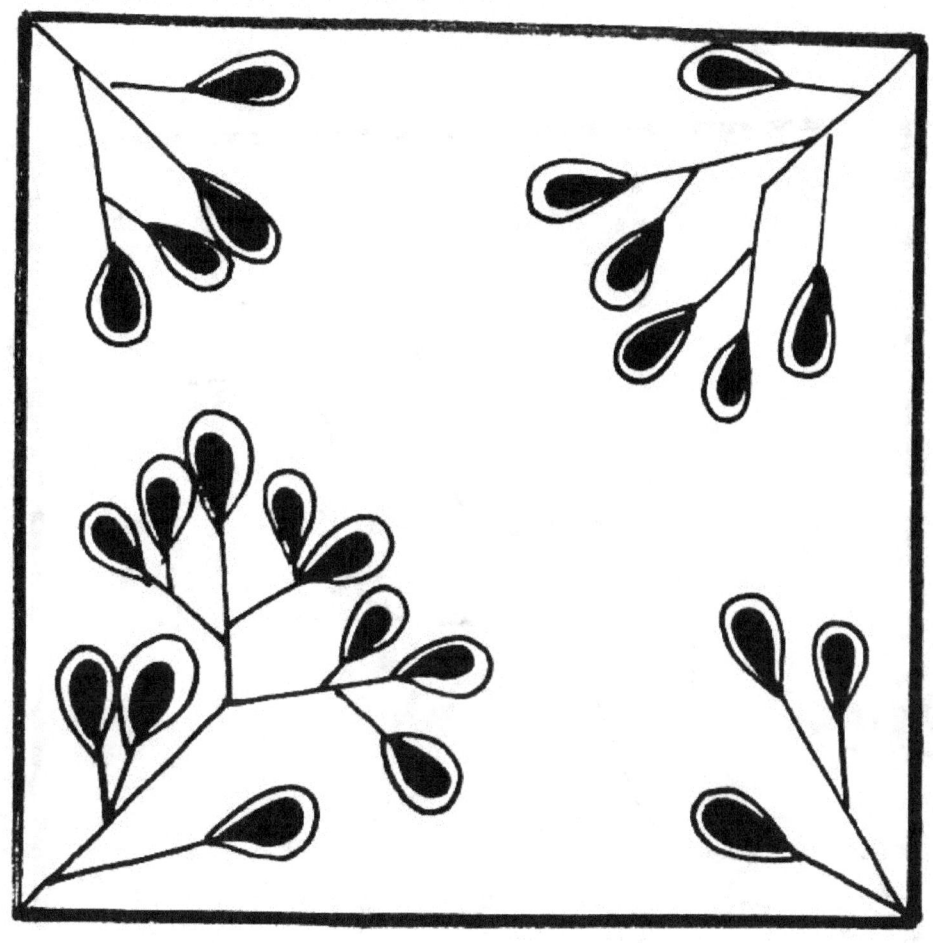

Pattern 4
Isry

Step 1

Draw a square on a sheet of paper.

Draw two parallel waves from the lower left corner to the upper right corner of the box, but the ends of the waves should meet at the corners.

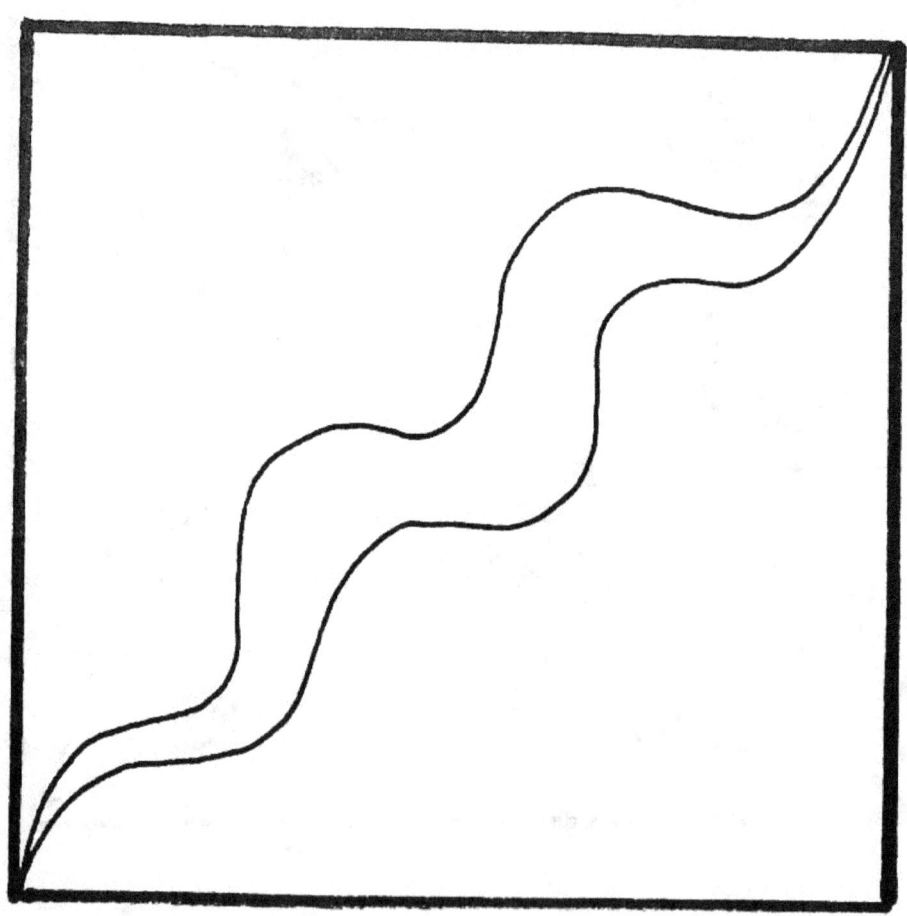

Step 2

Draw one more wave inside the previous one and fill it with ink as shown in the picture.

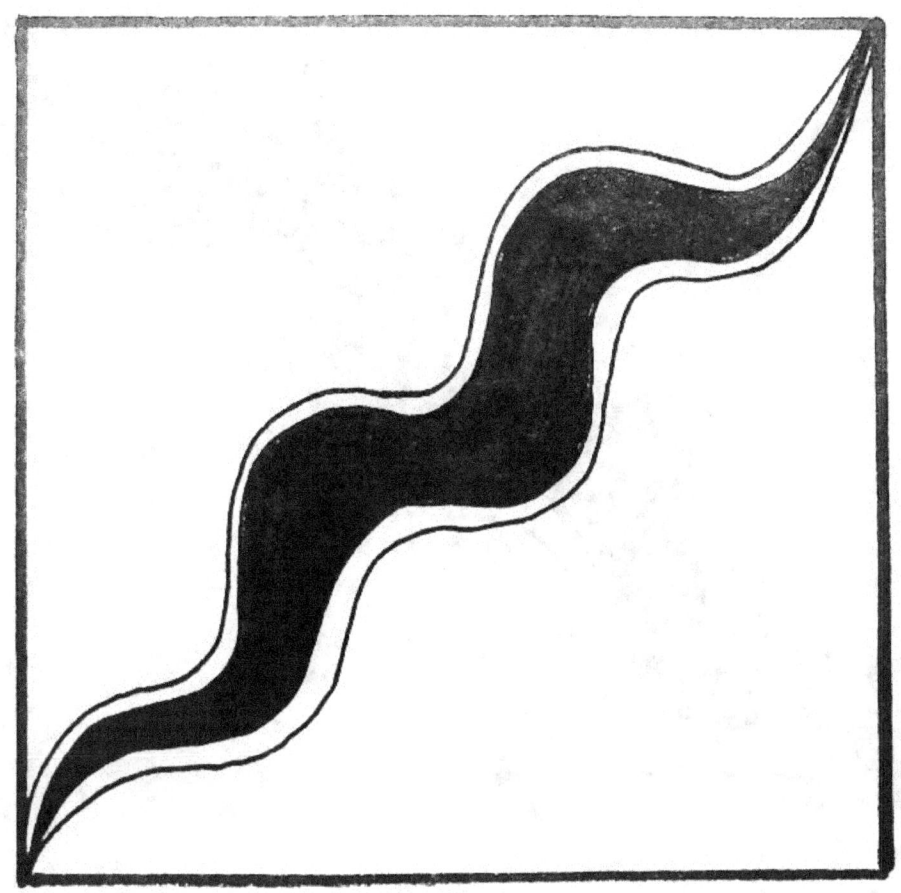

Step 3

Draw a few small circles along the both edges of the wave.

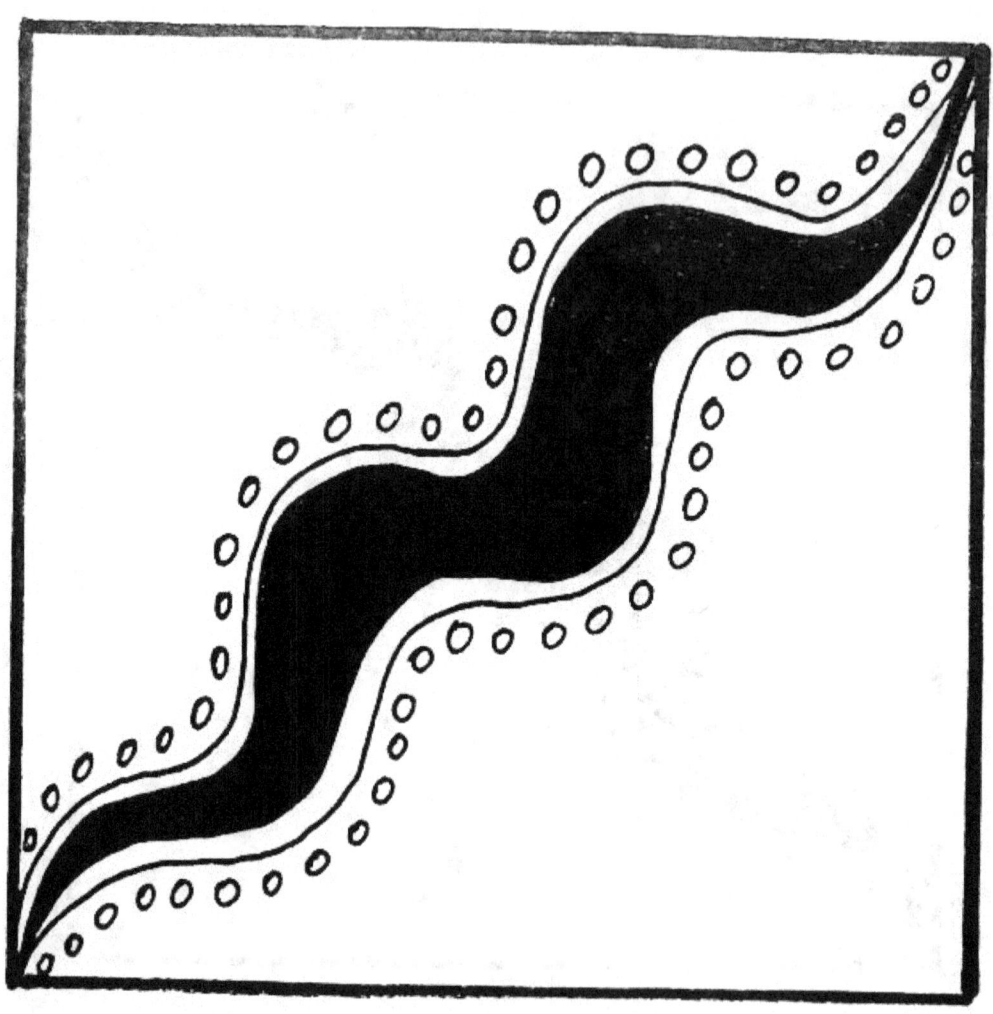

Step 4

Draw more waves in the box as shown in the picture.

The isry pattern is complete.

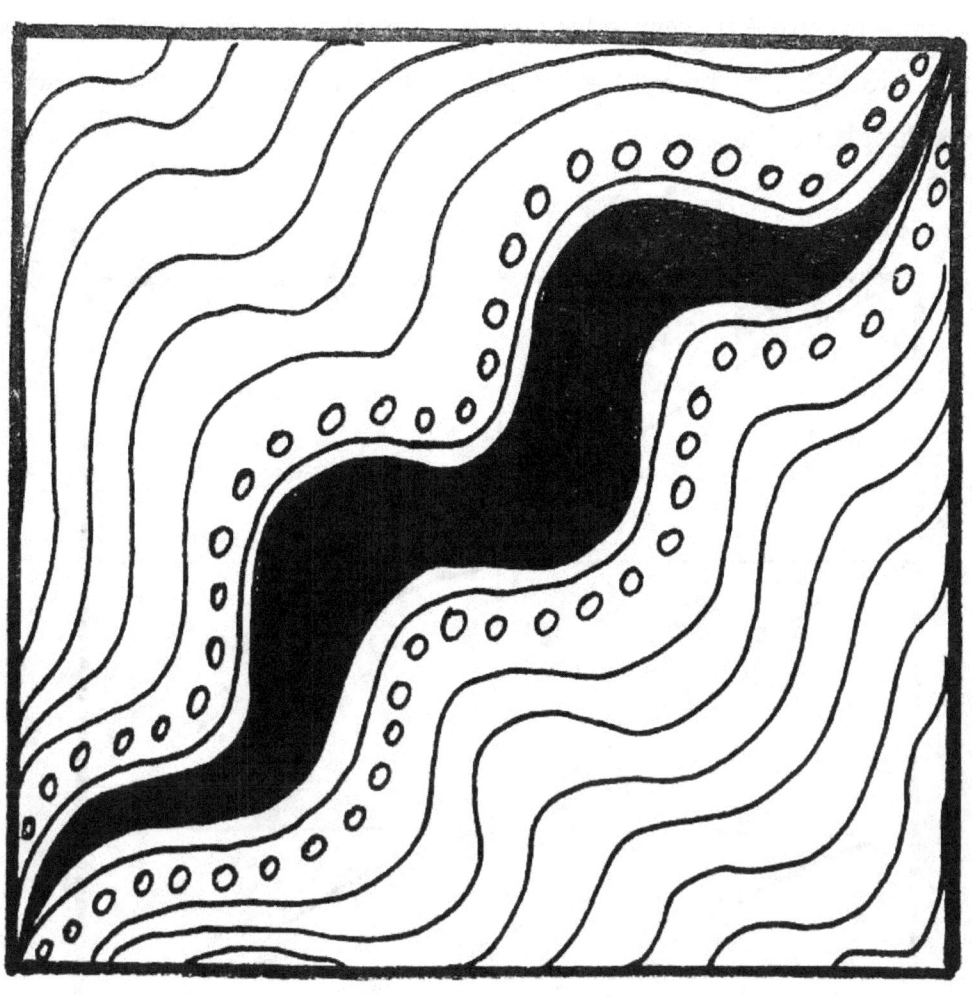

Pattern 5
Difky

Step 1

Draw a square on a sheet of paper.

Divide the box into six rectangles as shown in the picture. Draw a diagonal, but not straight, line from the top left corner to the lower right corner of each rectangle in the box.

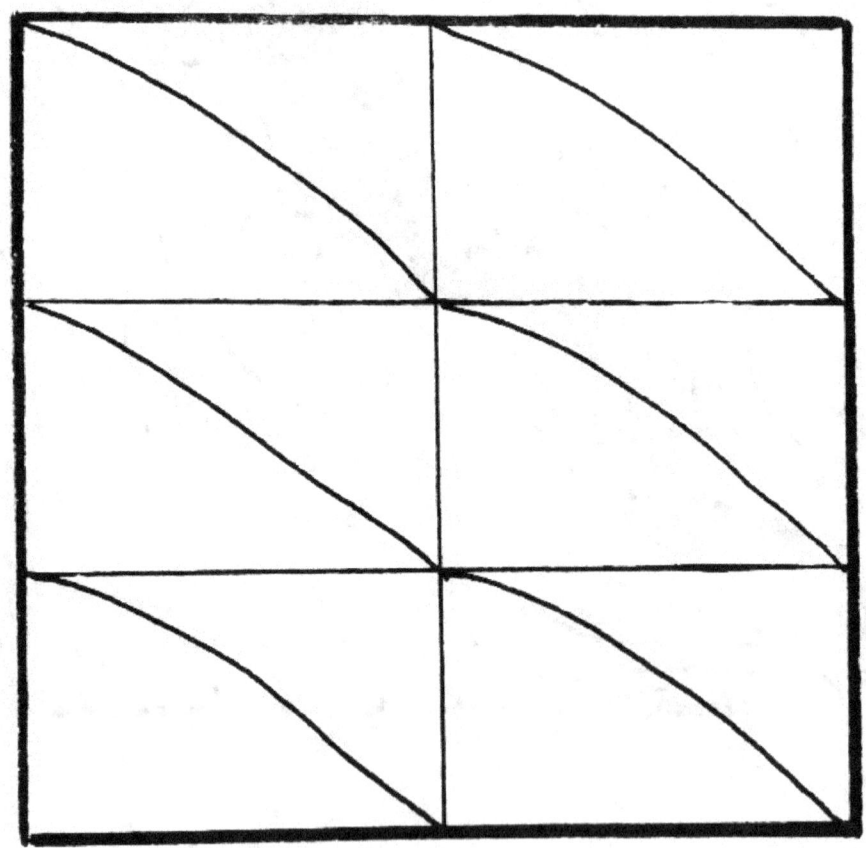

Step 2

Draw graduating ovals in the left side of each rectangle divided by the diagonals as shown in the picture. The smallest oval should be in the lower right corner and the biggest oval should be in the top right corner of the box.

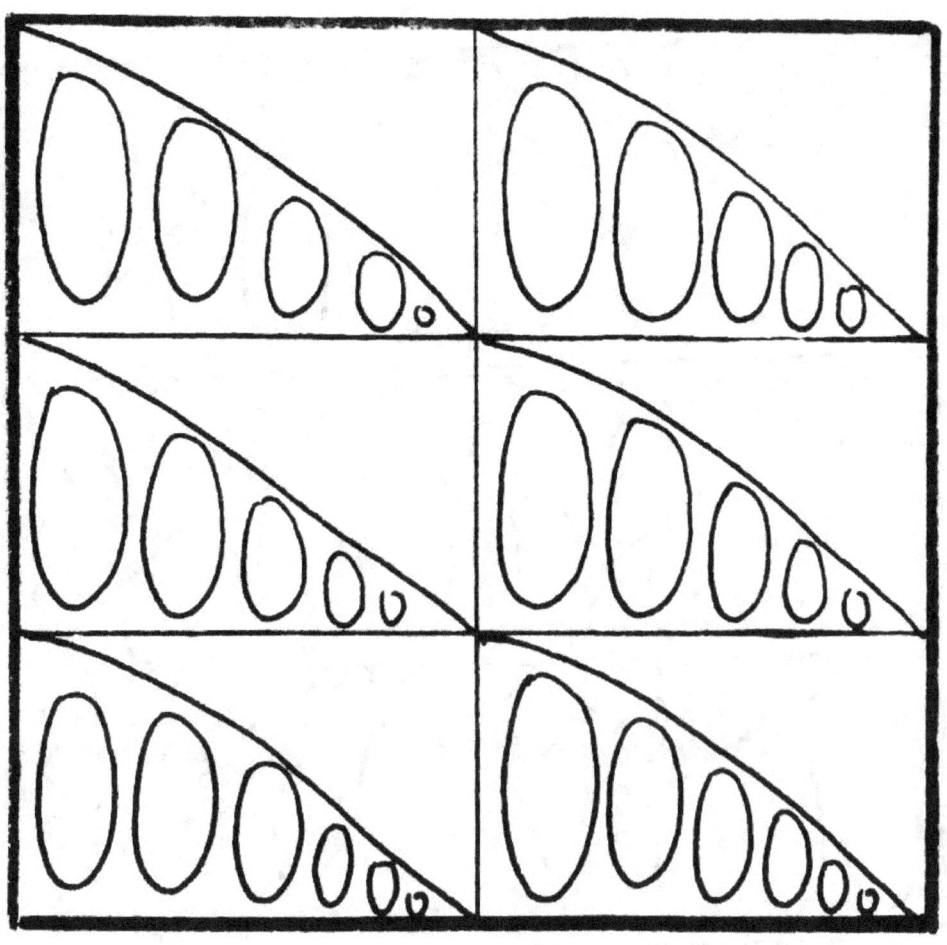

Step 3

In the right side of each triangle, draw a few vertical waves as shown in the picture.

The difky pattern is complete.

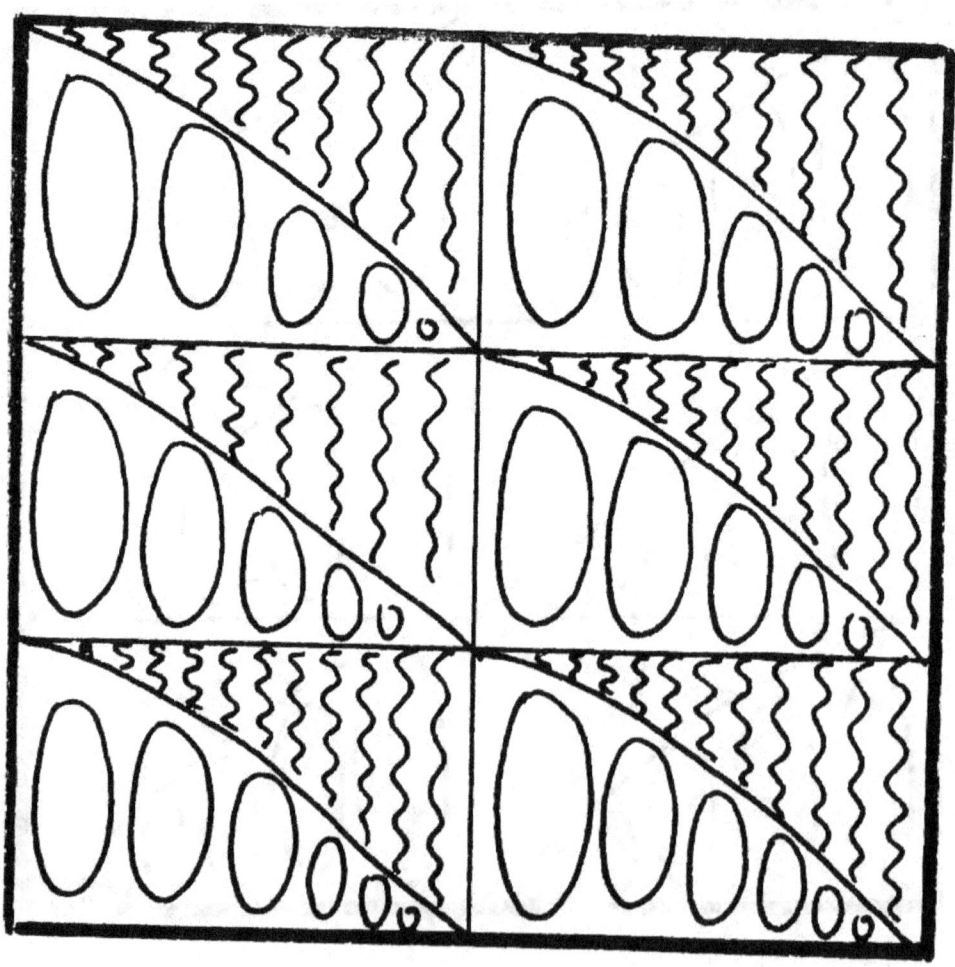

Pattern 6
Beu

Step 1

Draw a square on a sheet of paper.

Divide the box into five sets of four lines each, as shown in the picture.

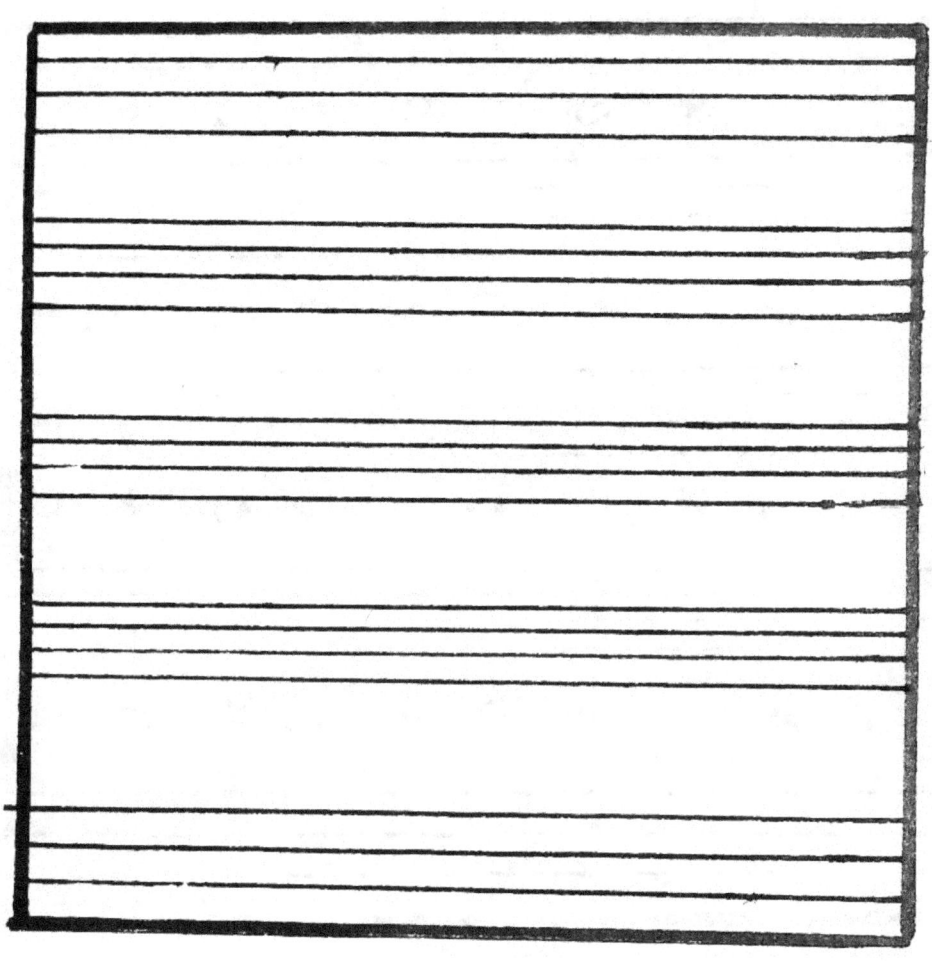

Step 2

In the margin that remains between these sets of lines, draw circles and star shapes alternatively.

The beu pattern is complete.

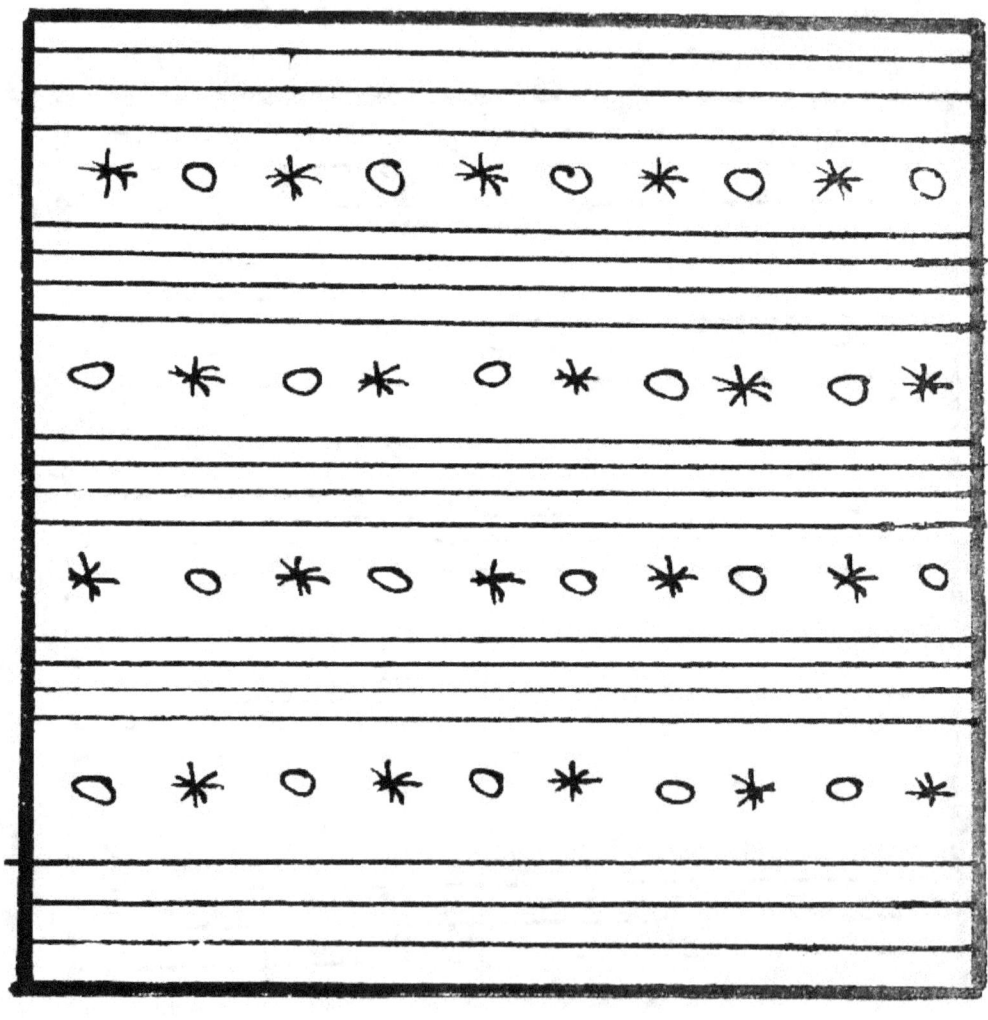

Pattern 7
Norl

Step 1

Draw a square on a sheet of paper.

Draw two small parallel diagonal lines in the top right corner of the box.

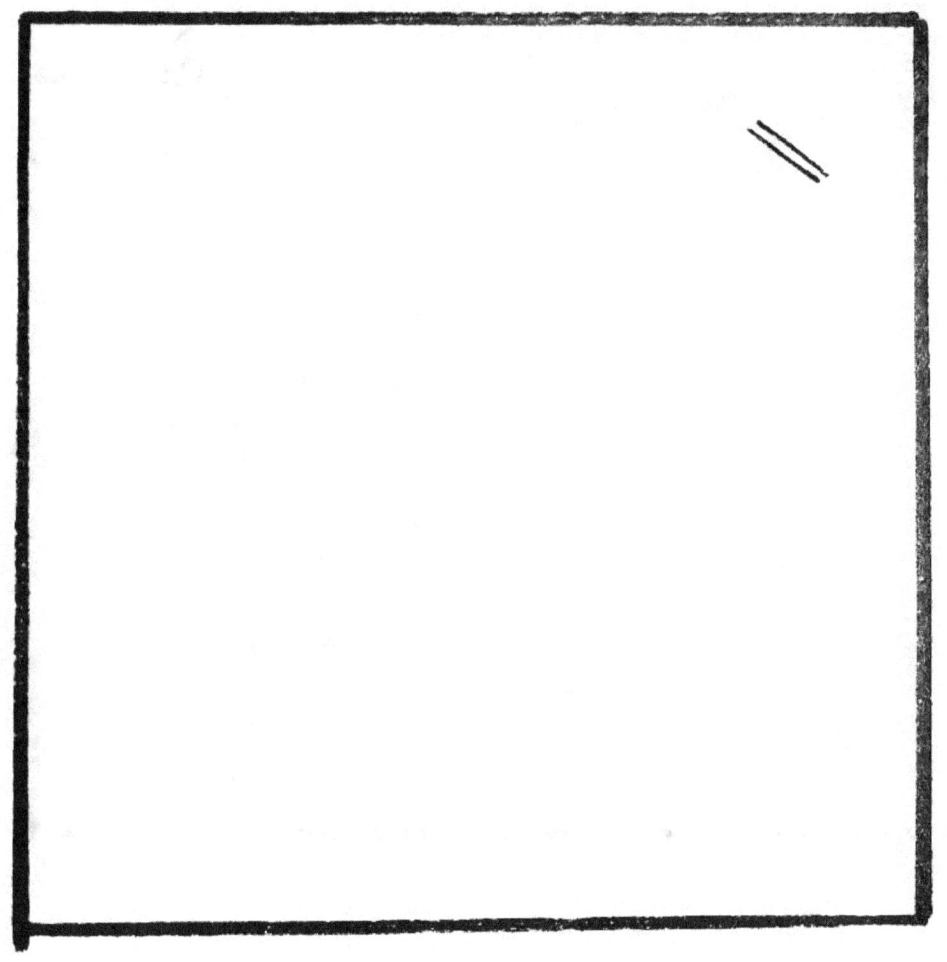

Step 2

Draw two semi circles on both sides of the parallel lines and draw a parallel semi-circle on the edge of the previous ones.

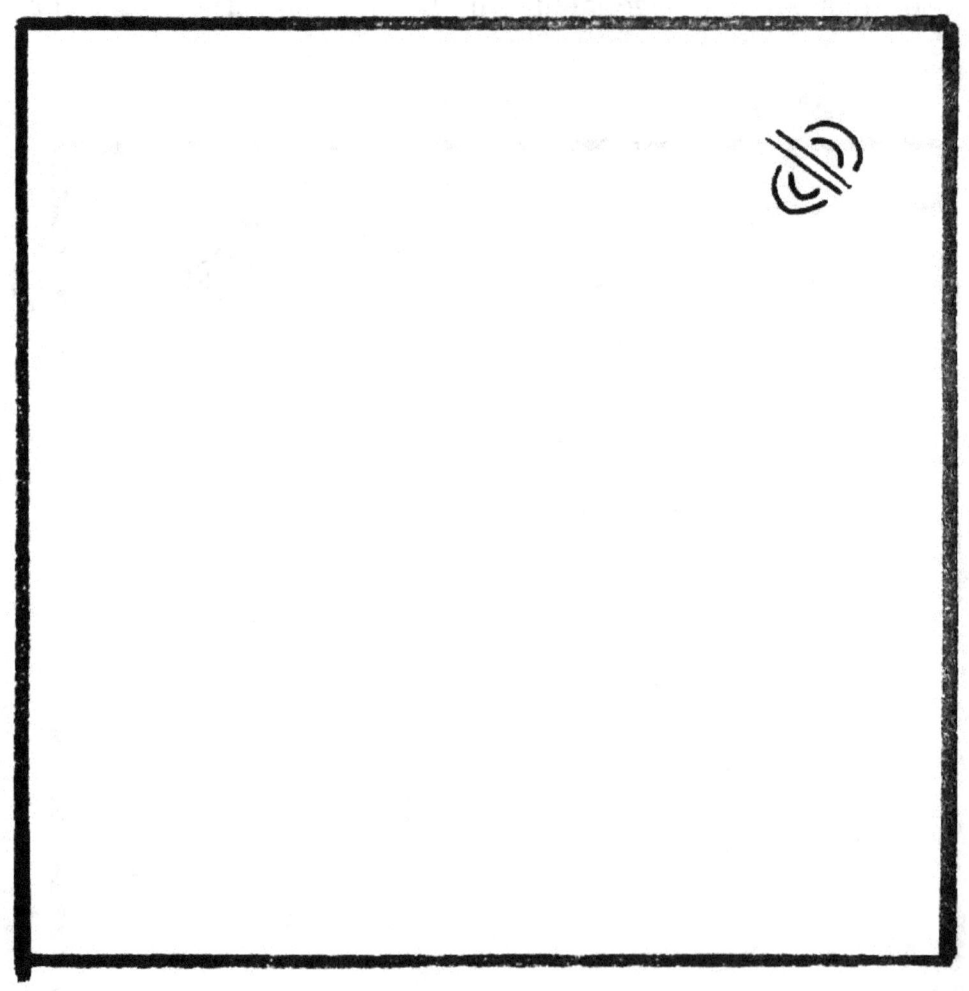

Step 3

Repeat step 1 and step 2 to draw similar patterns in the box in various directions.

The norl pattern is complete.

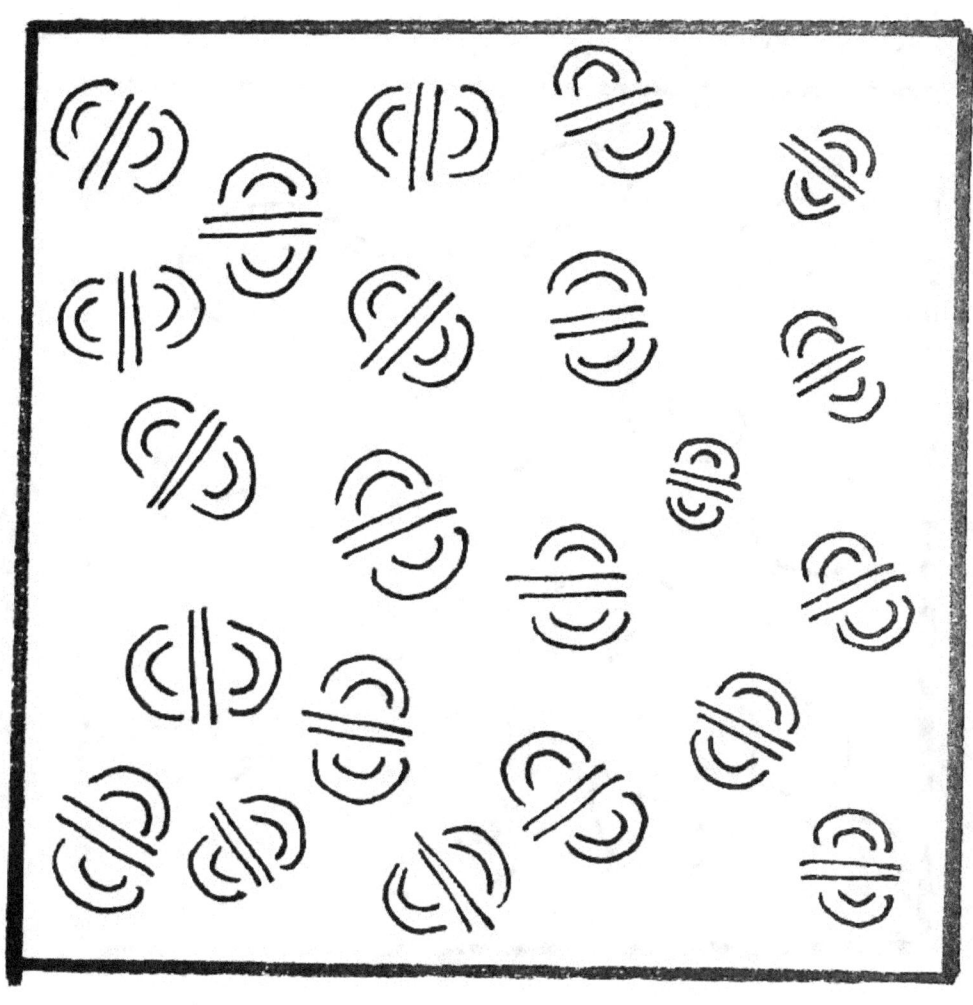

Pattern 8
Calcy

Step 1

Draw a square on a sheet of paper.

Draw a few twisted drop shapes in the box as shown in the picture.

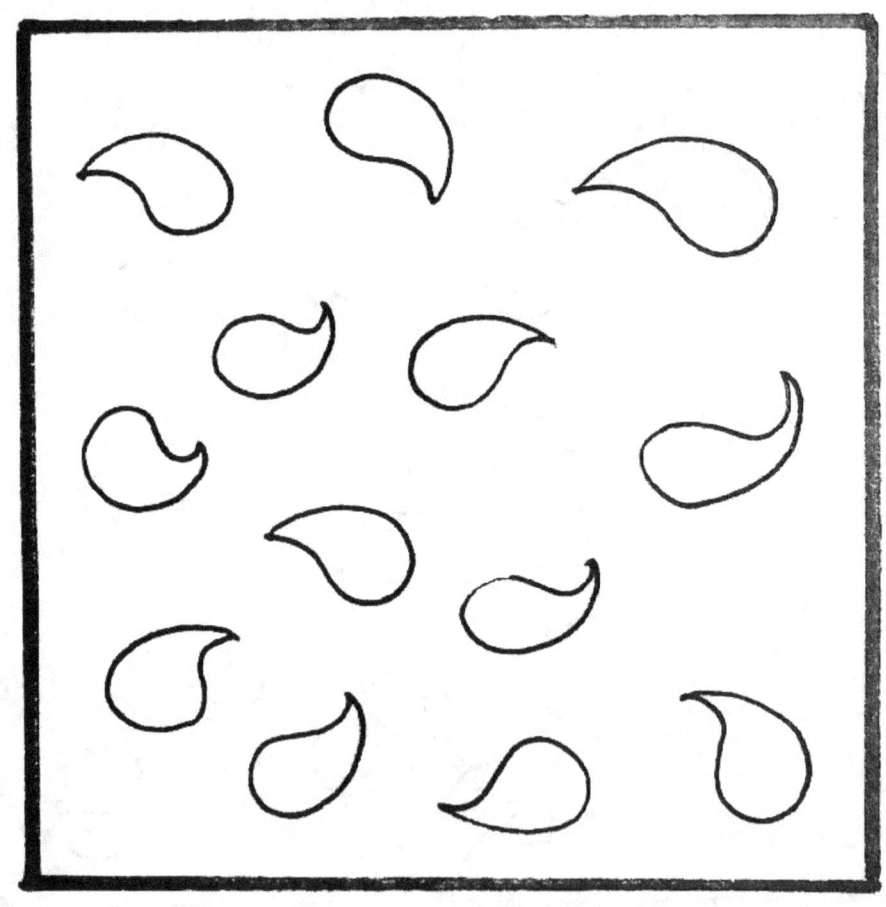

Step 2

Draw a few scallops in one of the drops. See the picture for reference.

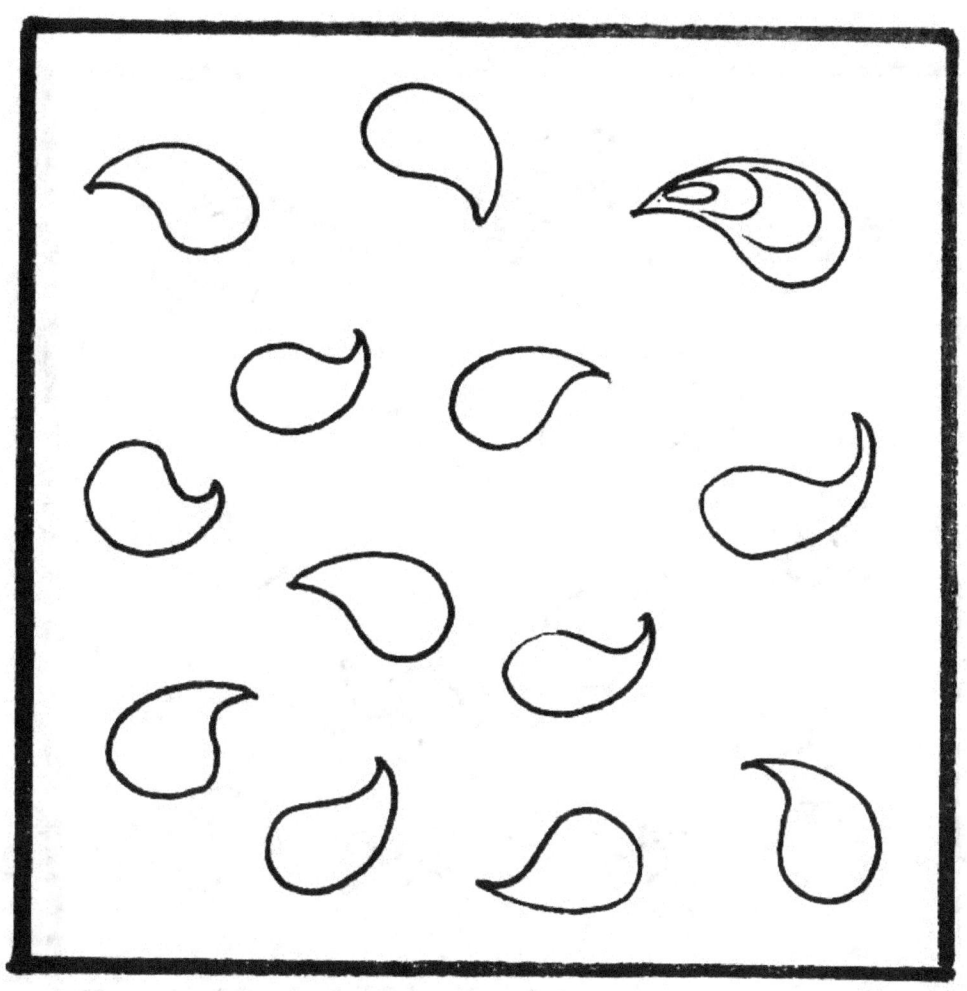

Step 3

Repeat step 2 for the remaining twisted drops.

The calcy pattern is complete.

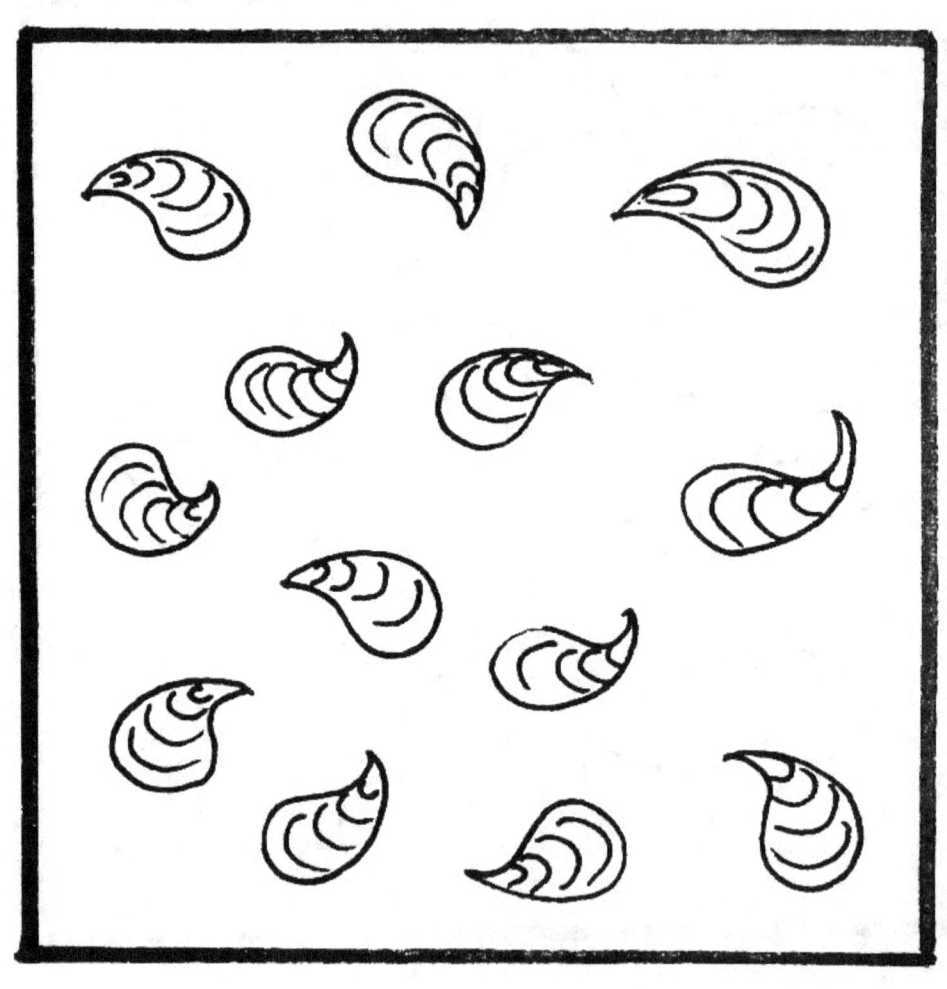

Pattern 9
Ethu

Step 1

Draw a square on a sheet of paper.

Divide the box into three unequal vertical sections as shown in the picture.

Step 2

In the middle section, draw three eye shapes using parallel lines. See the picture for reference.

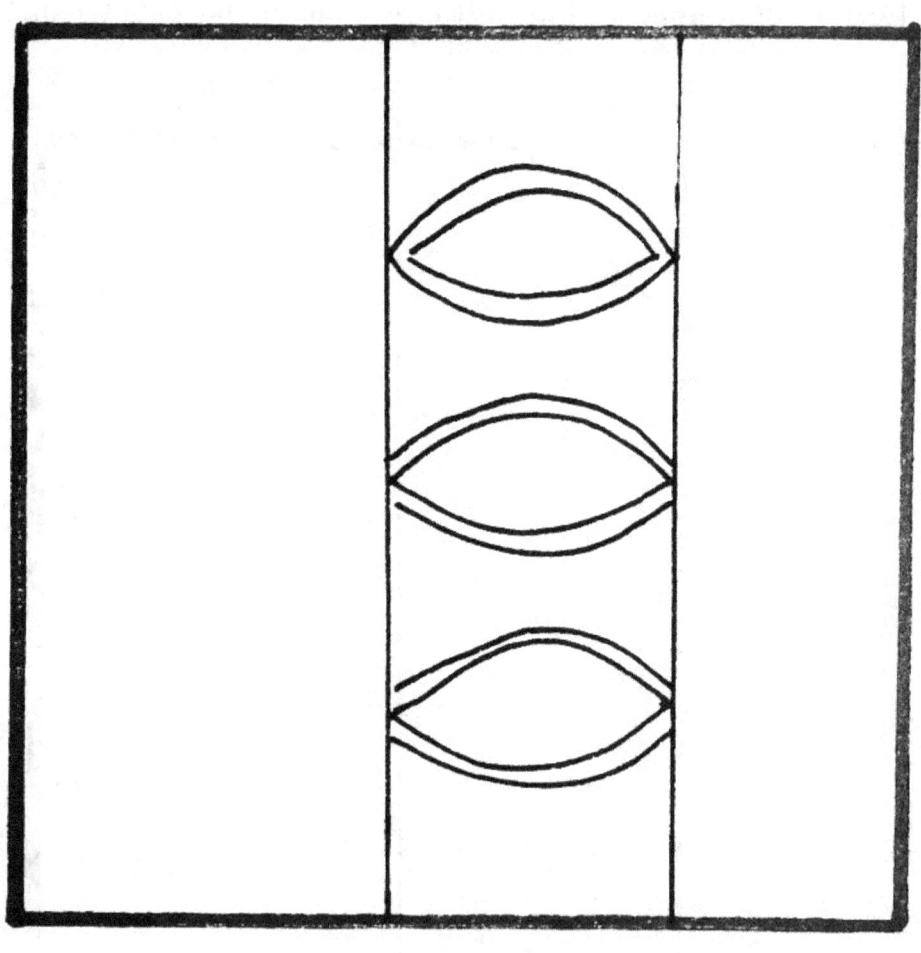

Step 3

Draw a few small circles in a horizontal line in the eye shapes.

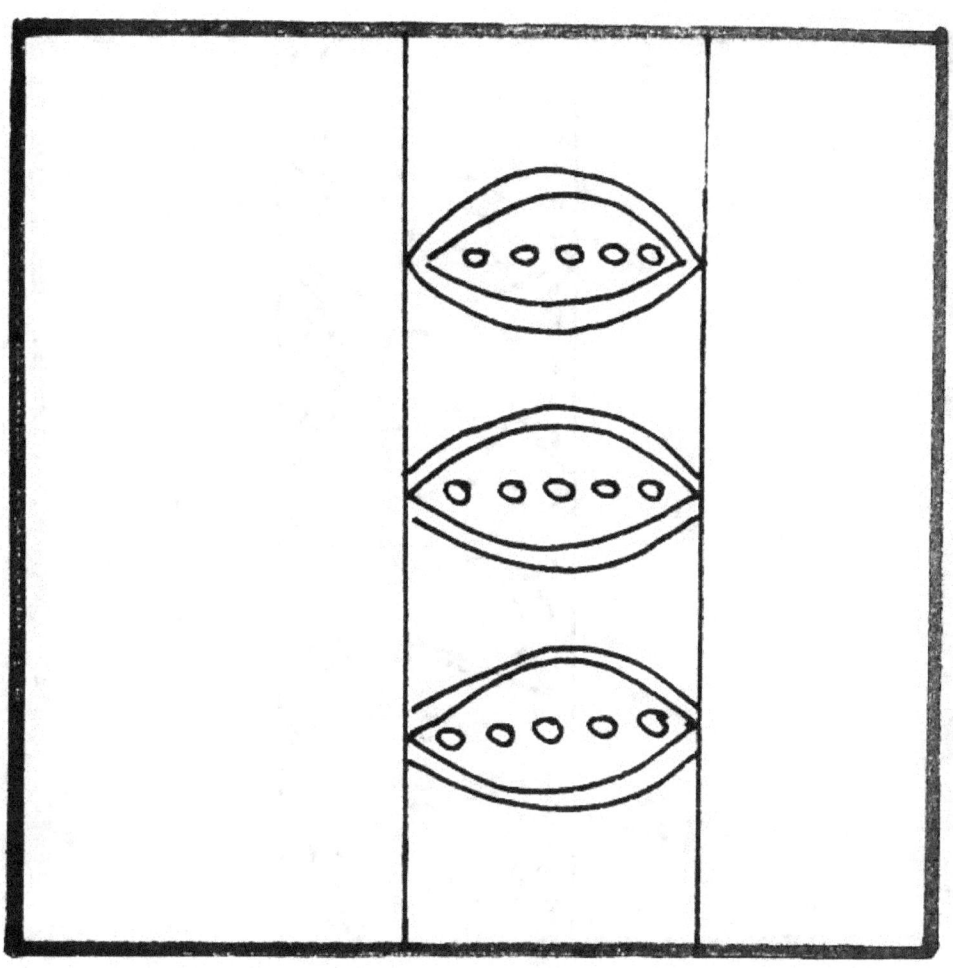

Step 4

Draw a few vertical lines along the inner edges of the middle section.

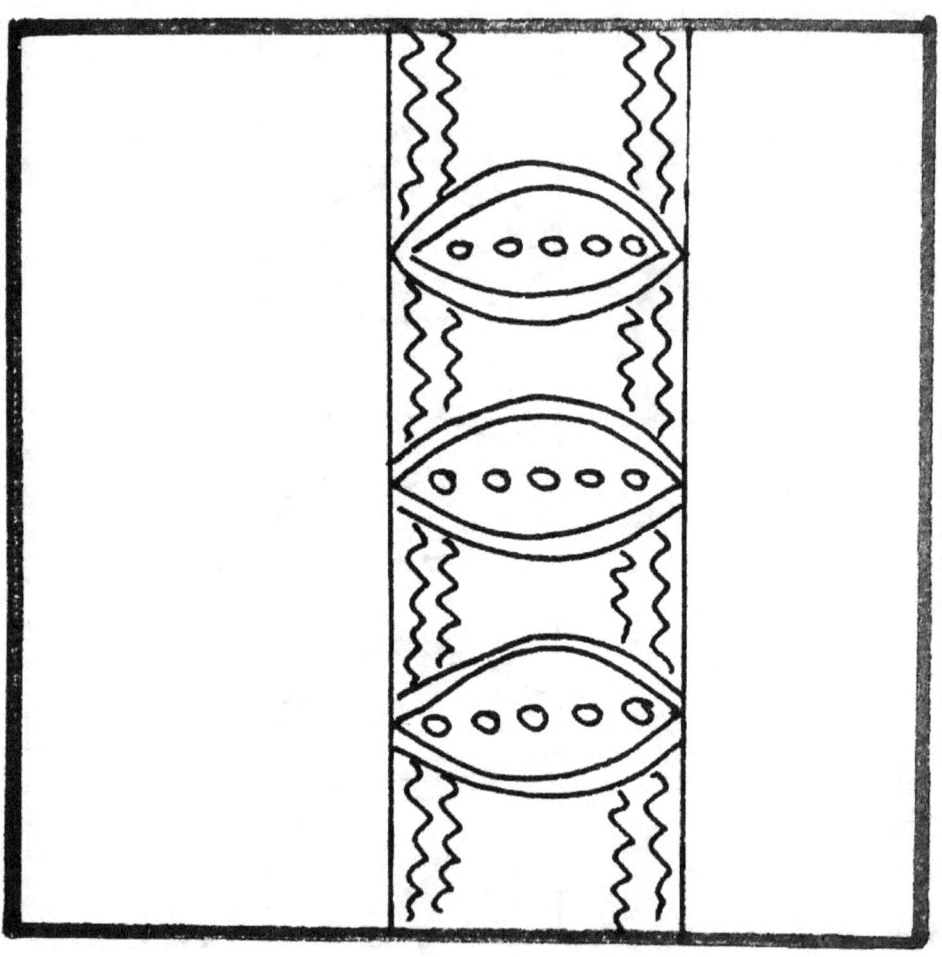

Step 5

In the remaining part of the middle section, draw a few parallel diagonal lines.

The ethu pattern is complete.

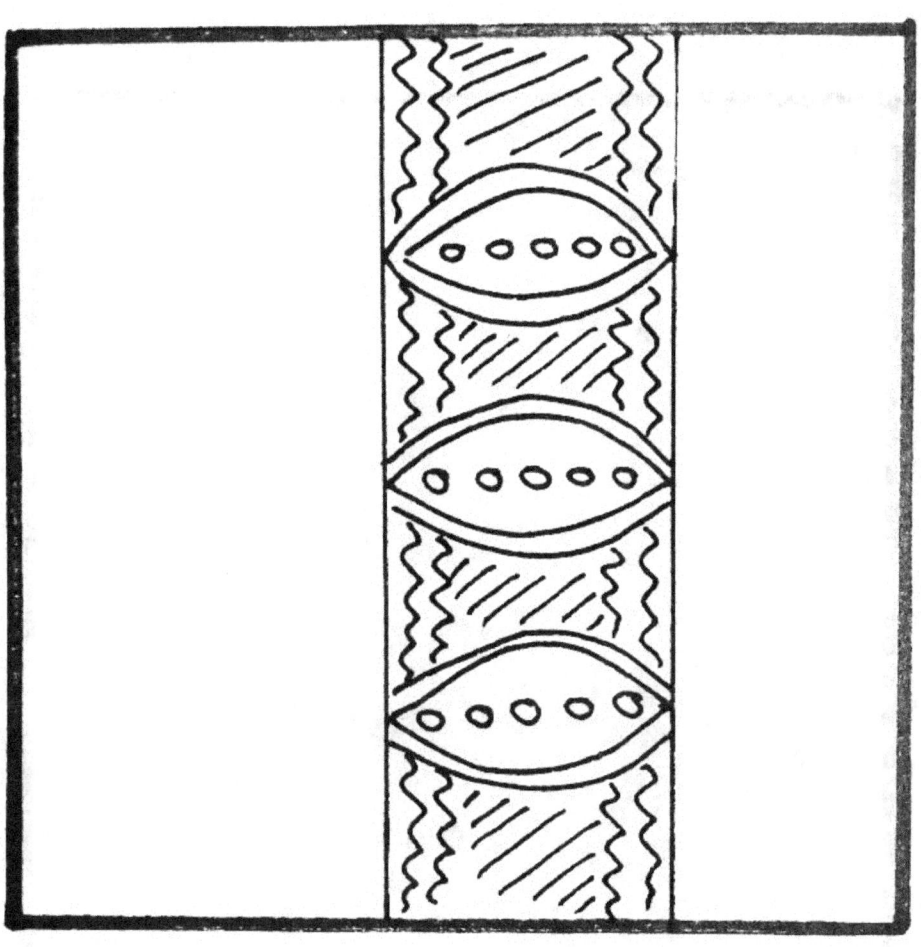

Pattern 10
Ably

Step 1

Draw a square on a sheet of paper.

Draw a few bullets in the box.

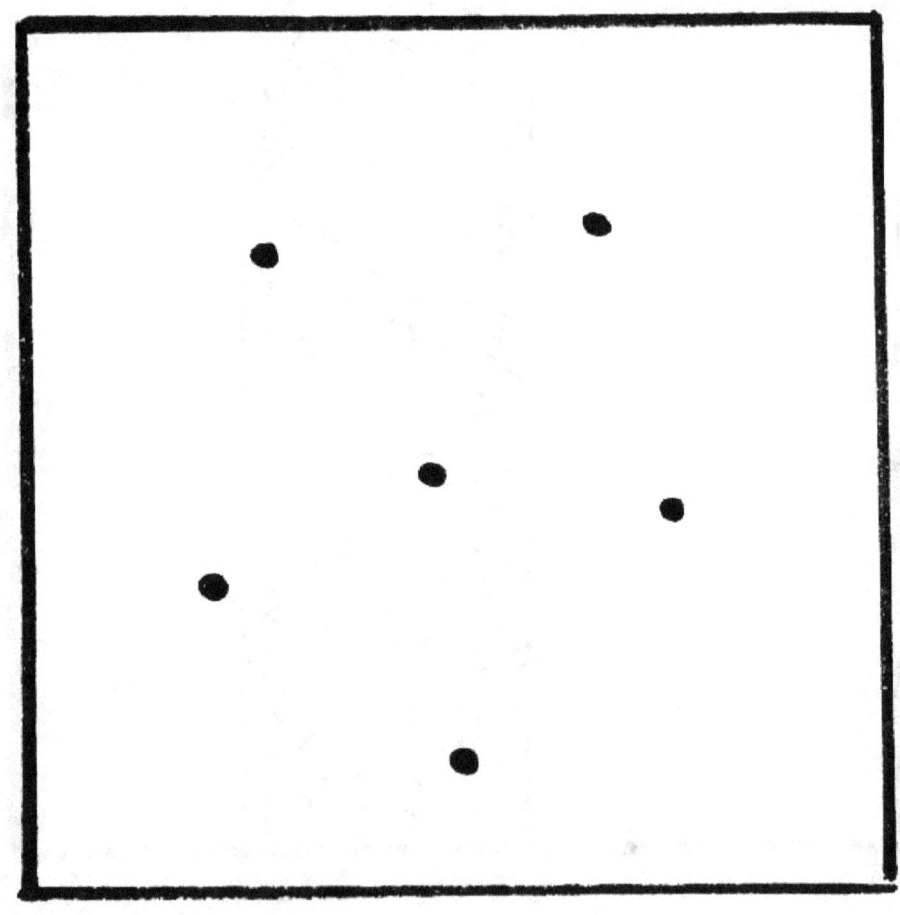

Step 2

Draw the flowers using the bullets drawn in the previous steps.

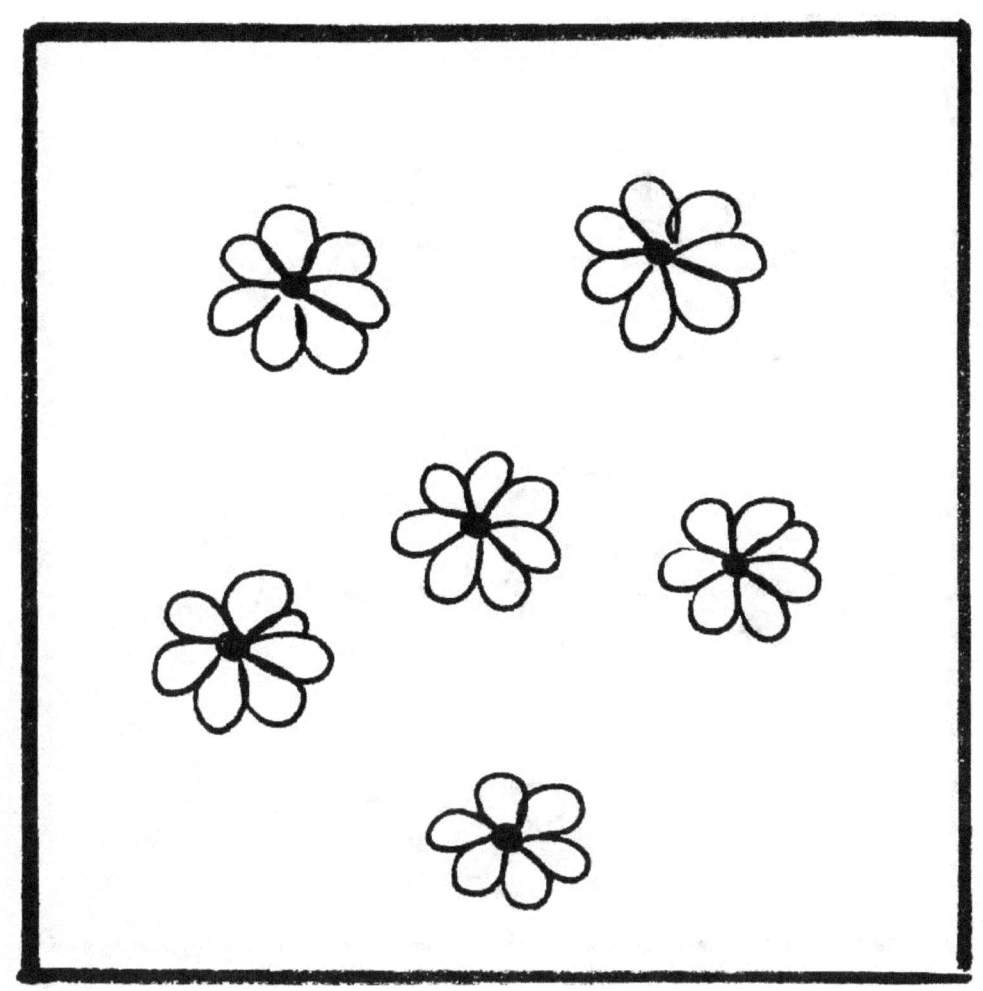

Step 3

Draw a few small twisted drop shapes around the flowers.

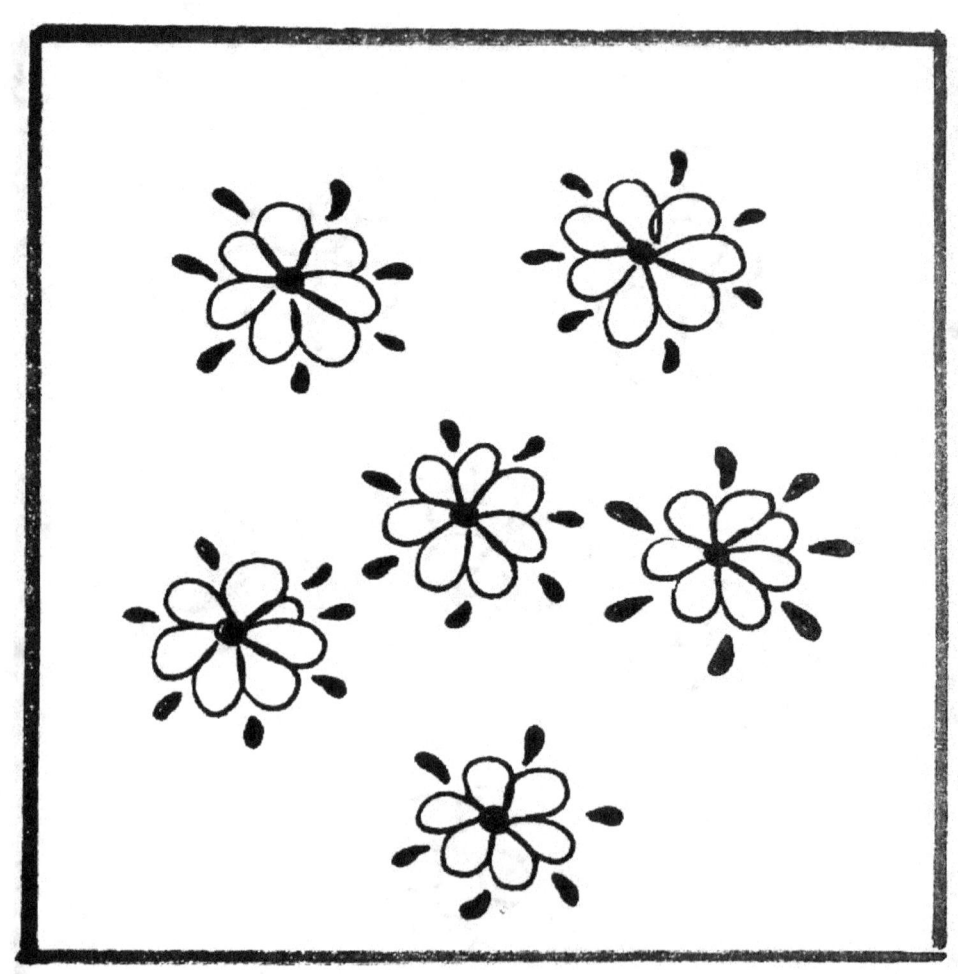

Step 4

Draw a few small circles in the remaining section of the box.
The ably pattern is complete.

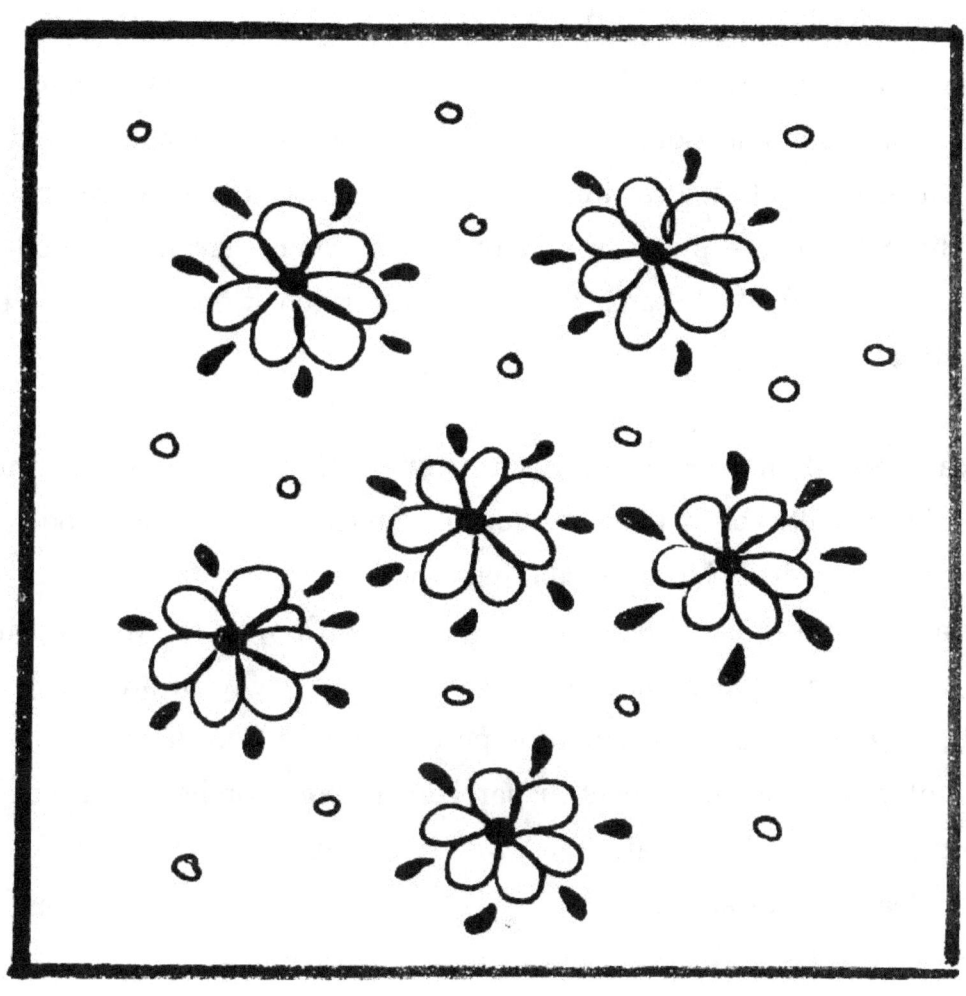

Chapter 3
Drawings created from Zen Doodle patterns

Now that you have learnt all the patterns in this book, it is time to utilize them in real applications. When we draw a pattern, we do not have to think much about its application. However, once you create it, you automatically start thinking about the drawings where you can use your new creations. In fact, the patterns are put to use at their best when they are applied in a drawing. Individual designs do not hold much importance in their respective boxes.

You can create Zen Doodle patterns any time you want. Even when you are sitting in the metro or by the lakeside, you can carry your drawing book and a pen or a pencil and start scribbling whenever you want. You can take inspiration from things around you- a water bottle with the words printed on it, the designs of your cat's fur, the teeth of your dog, your own hands, the design of your ring in your hand, the perfume bottle kept in your room, the shape of your cabinet, a beautiful jar kept in your kitchen, or a stack of magazines in the lobby of an office. Anything can inspire you provided you want to learn from such things.

Now let us start drawing a few illustrations using the patterns given in the previous chapter.

Drawing 1
Bear

Step 1

Draw the basic outline of the bear as shown in the picture.

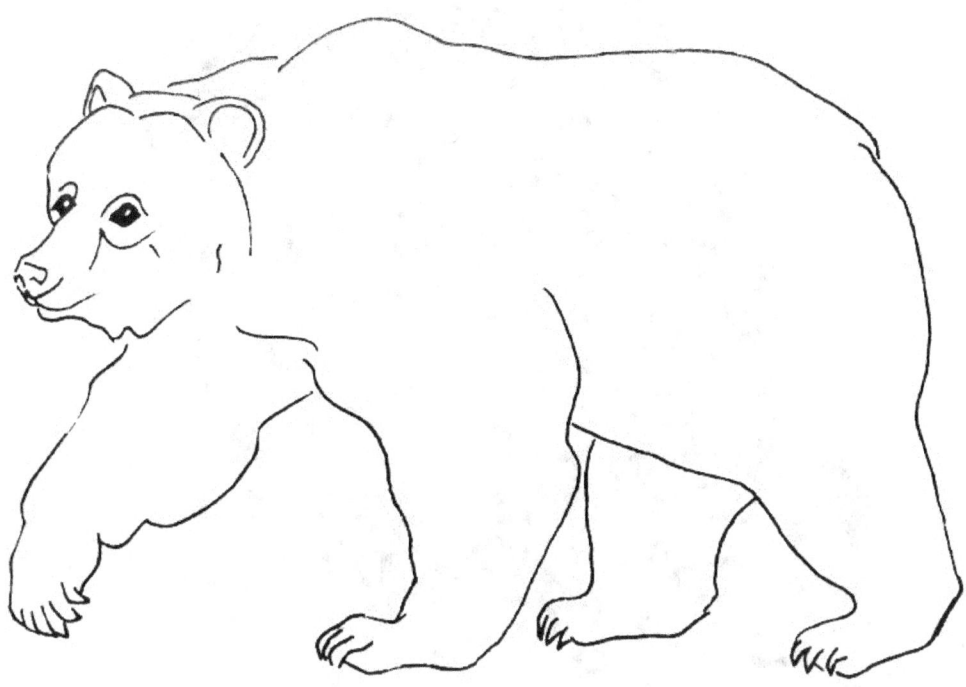

Step 2

Draw the galem and abbly pattern in the face of the bear.

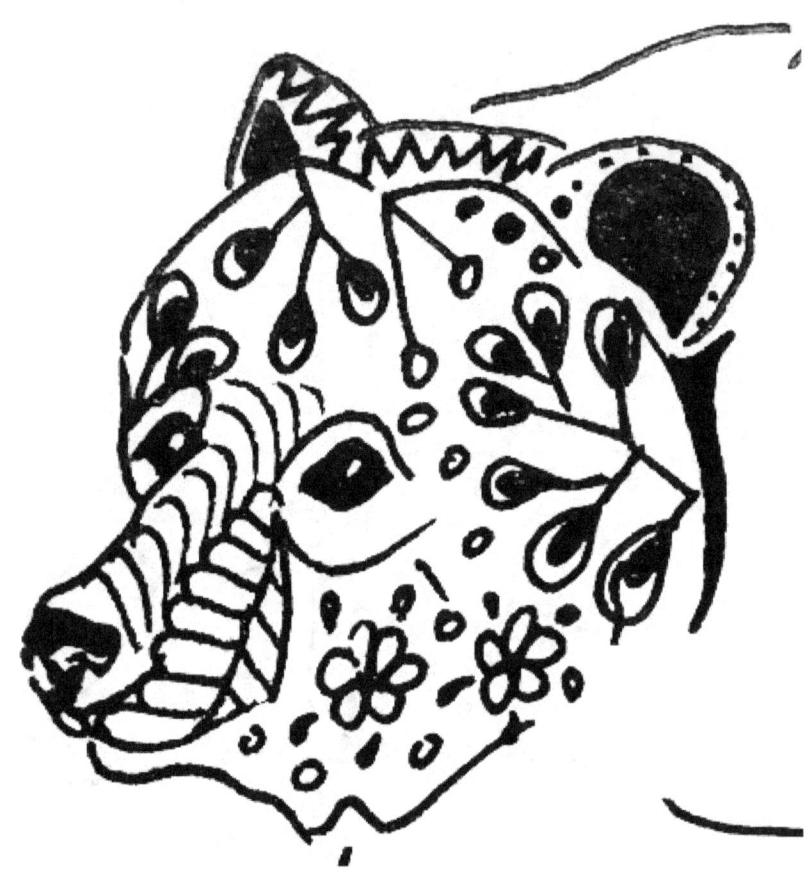

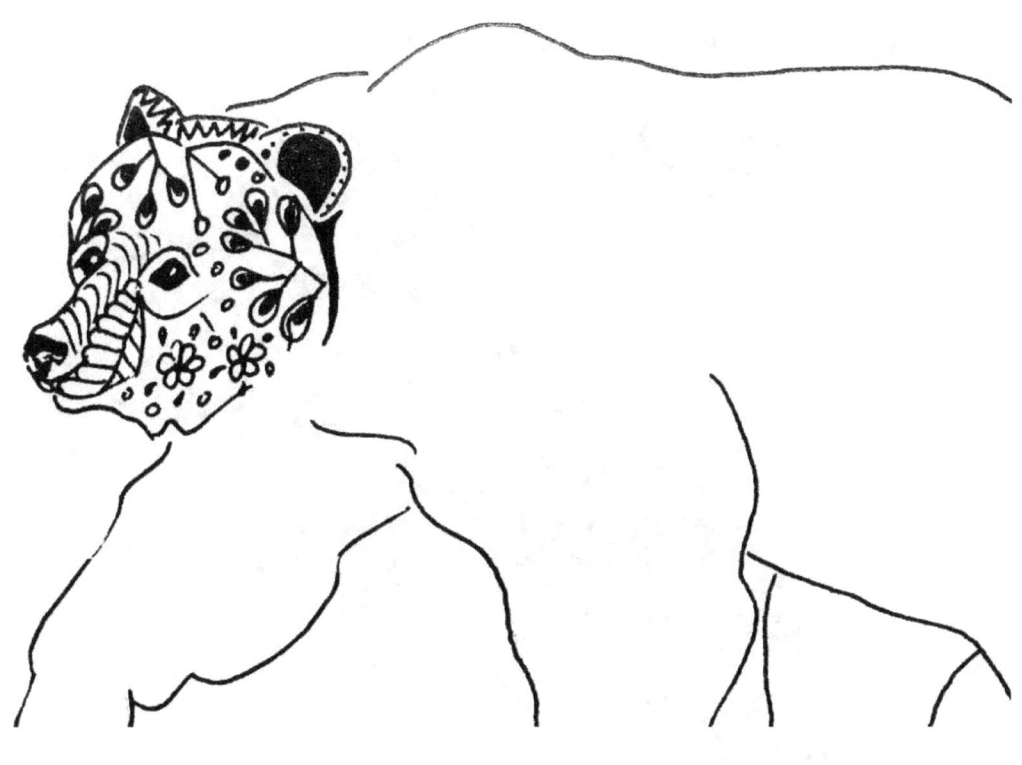

Step 3

Draw a combination of ethu and scallops in the front leg of the bear.

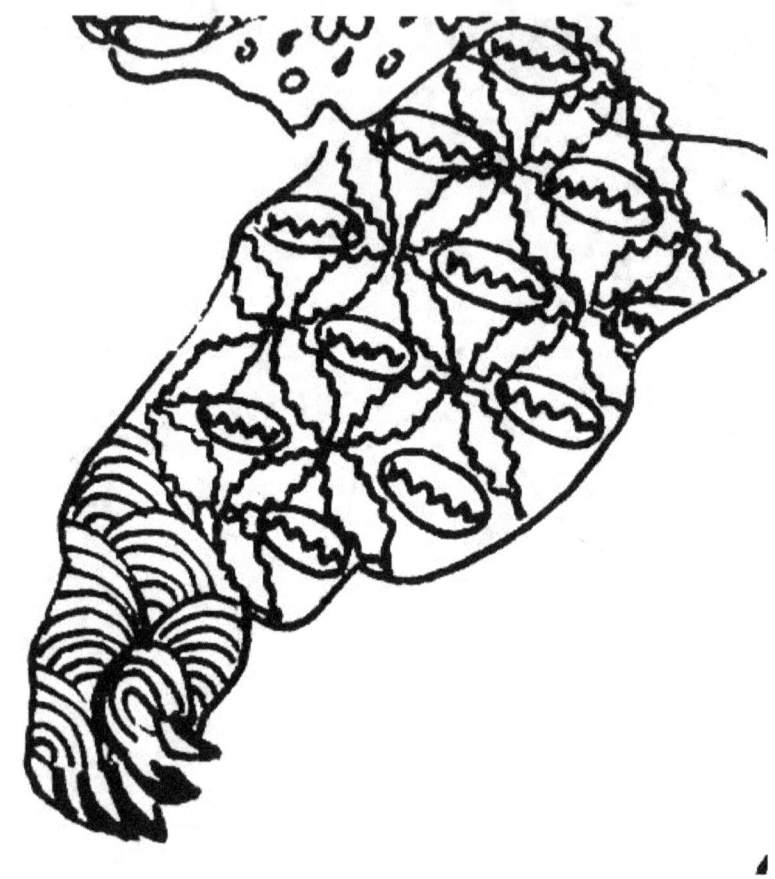

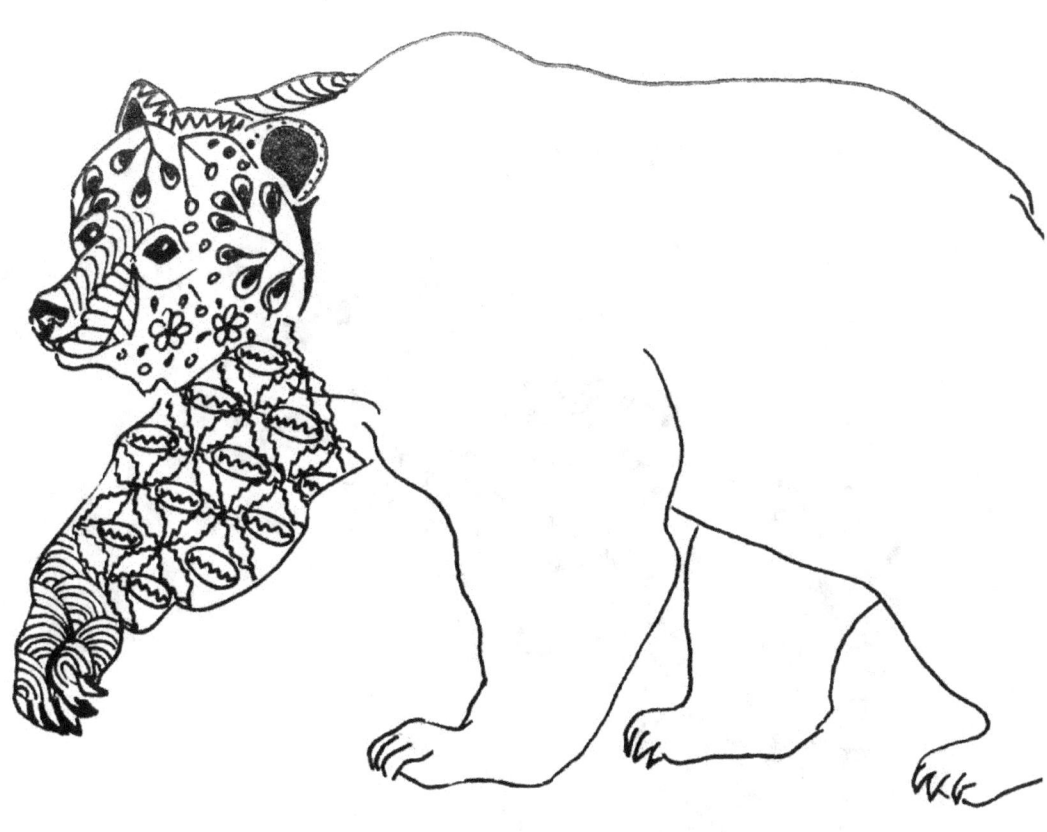

Step 4

Draw flub pattern in the upper portion of the bear's body.

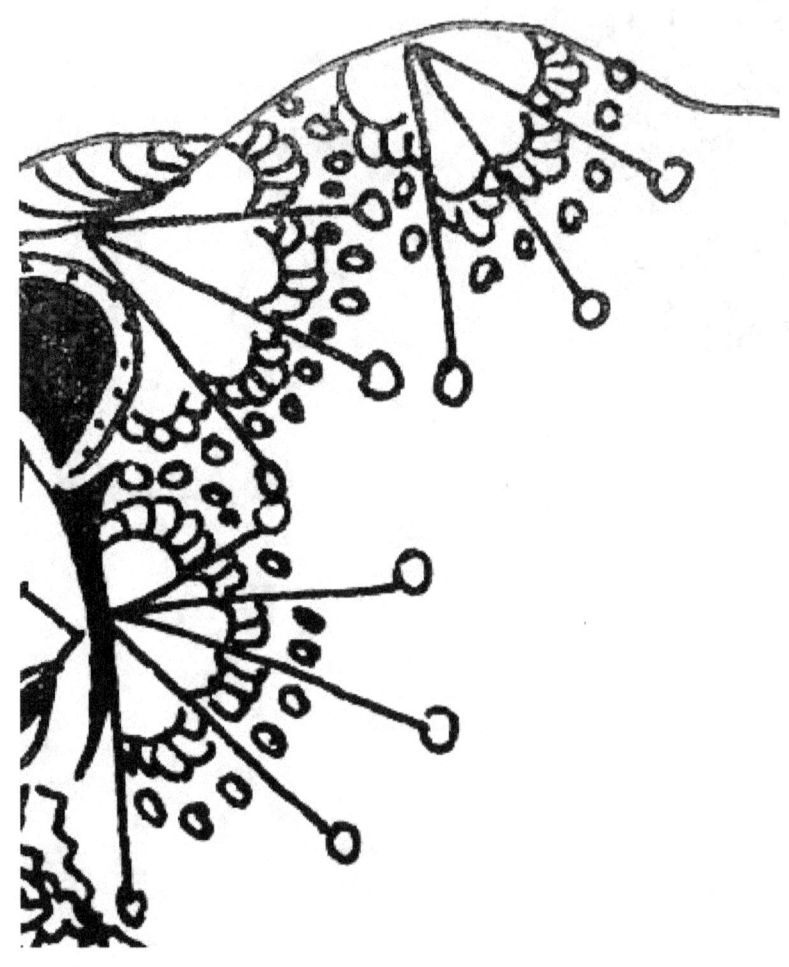

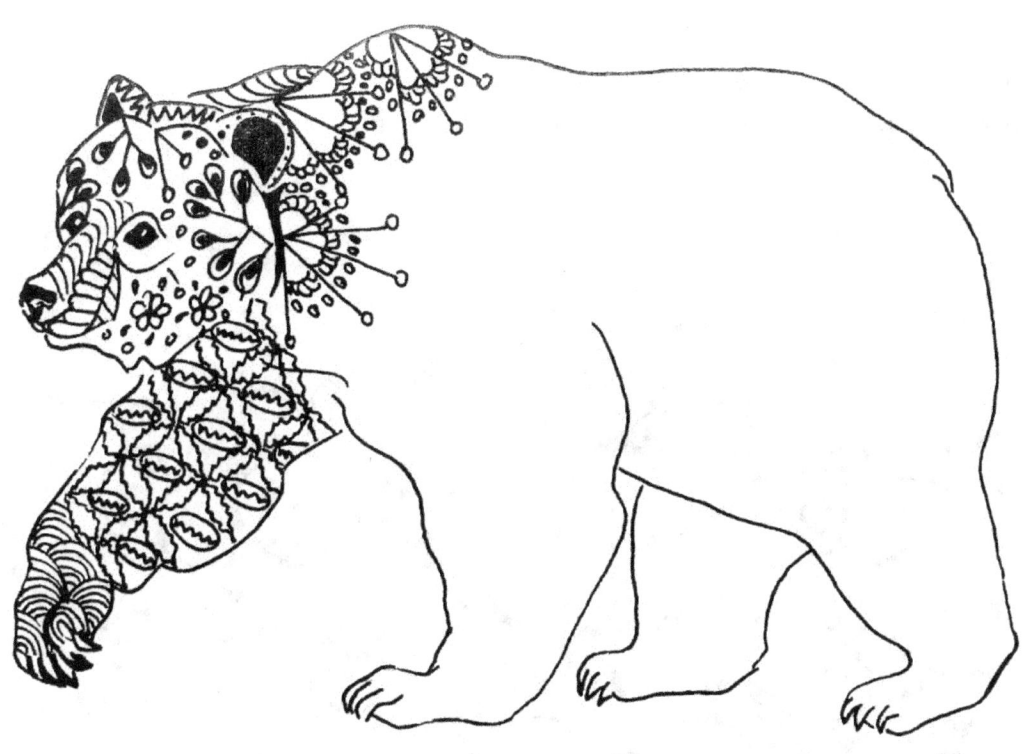

Step 5

Draw calcy pattern close to the club pattern.

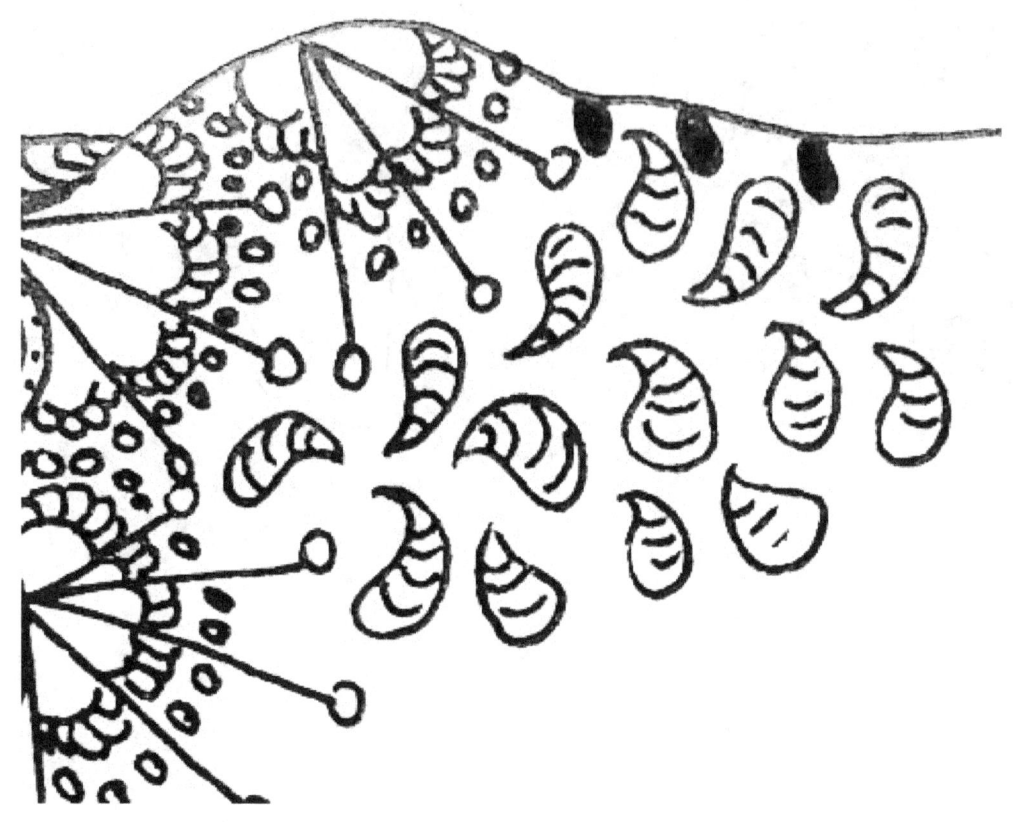

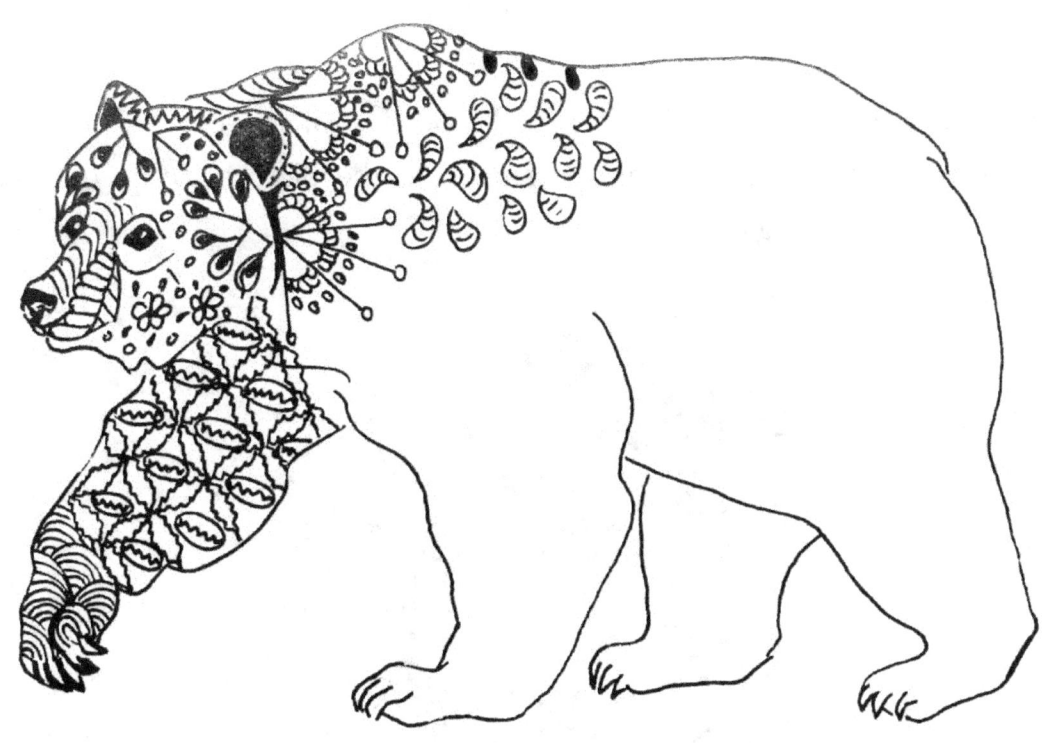

Step 6

Draw a few crossing lines in the middle portion of the bear's body and spread a few dots around them as shown in the picture. Draw the beu pattern in the front leg of the bear.

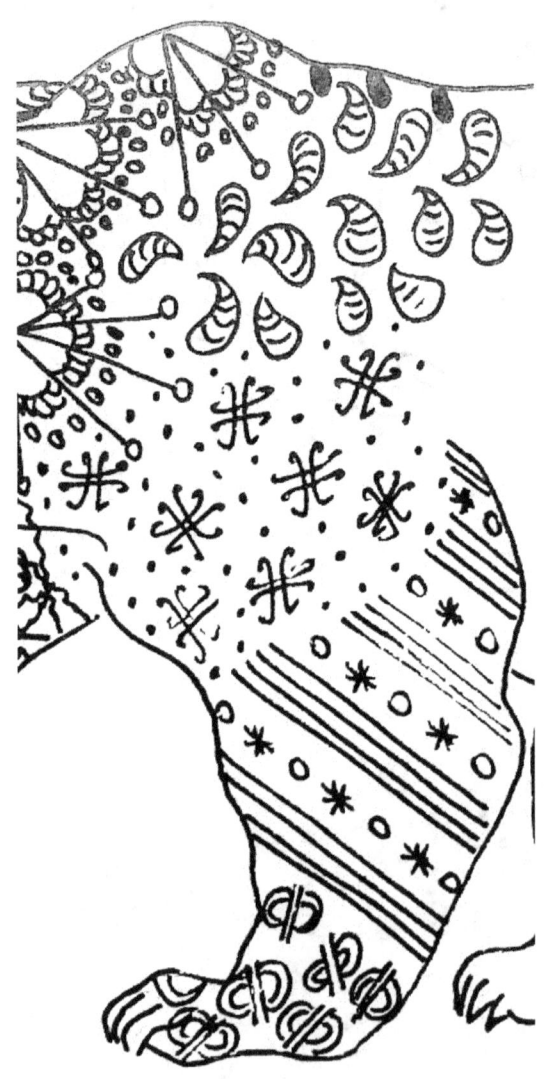

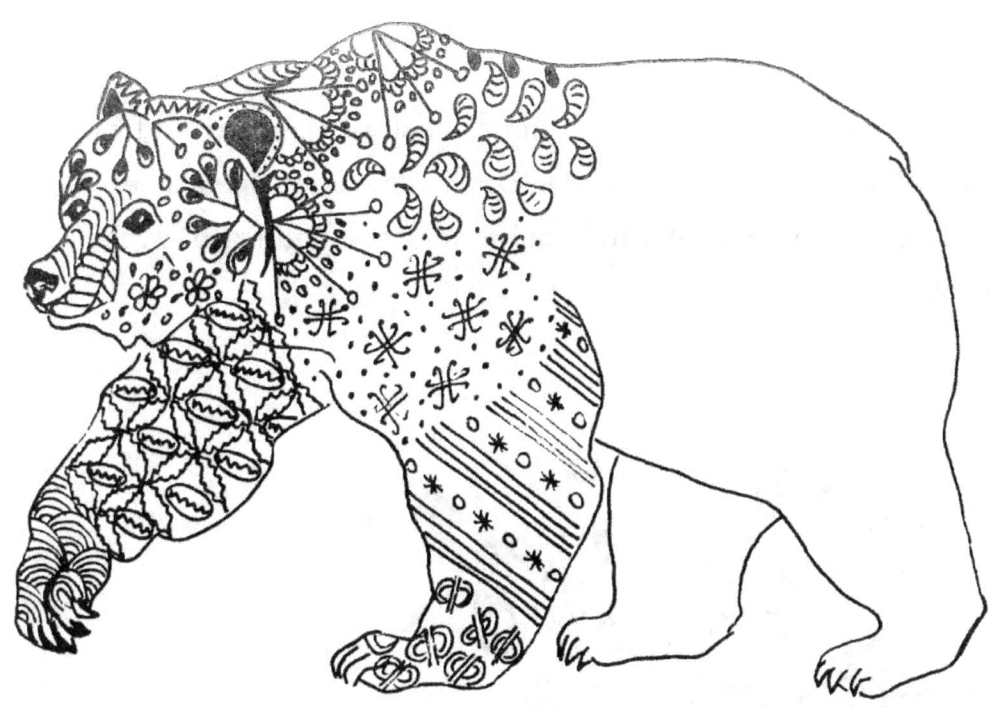

Step 7

Draw a few inverted arcs in the upper back of the bear and draw a few diagonal lines along the semi-circle. Draw a few flower petals between these lines. This pattern is similar to benif pattern you had learnt in the previous chapter.

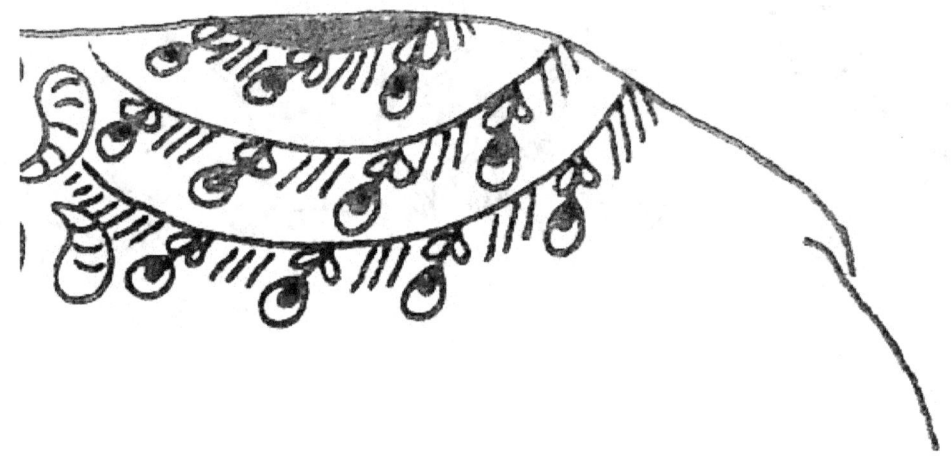

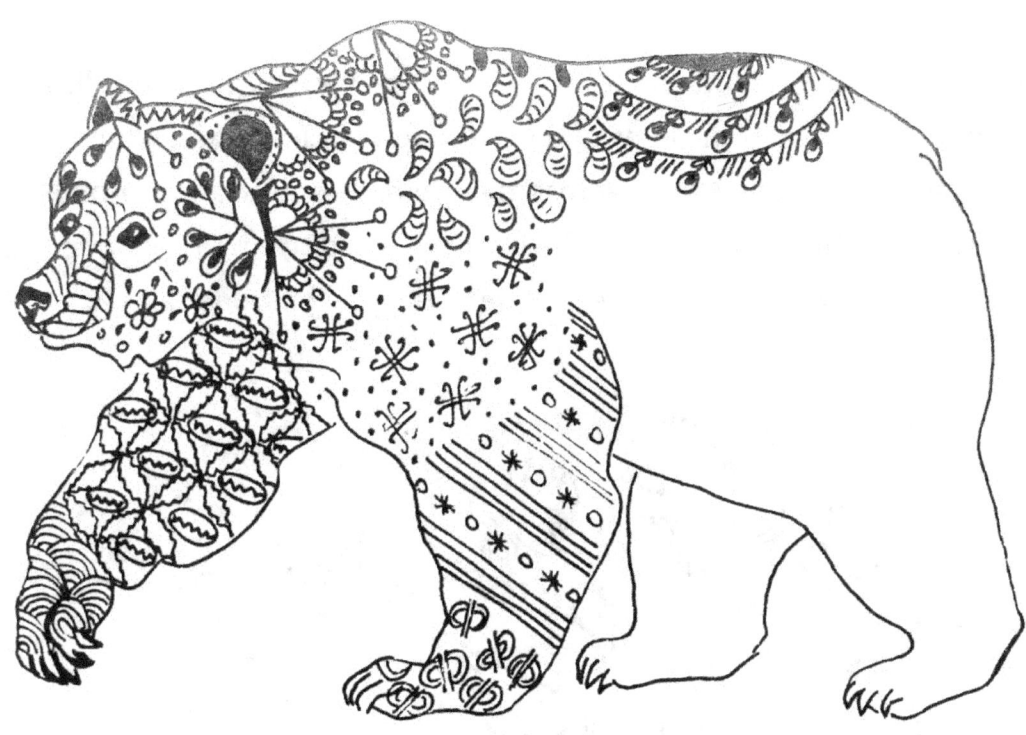

Step 8

Draw the isry pattern in the middle portion of the body. Draw a few diagonal lines in the posterior of the body and insert a few circles between them. Pass through a set of parallel lines across these circles and draw two bulbs on each side of the lines. You might have learnt this pattern in the previous part of this book. Draw the abbly pattern close to the previous one as well.

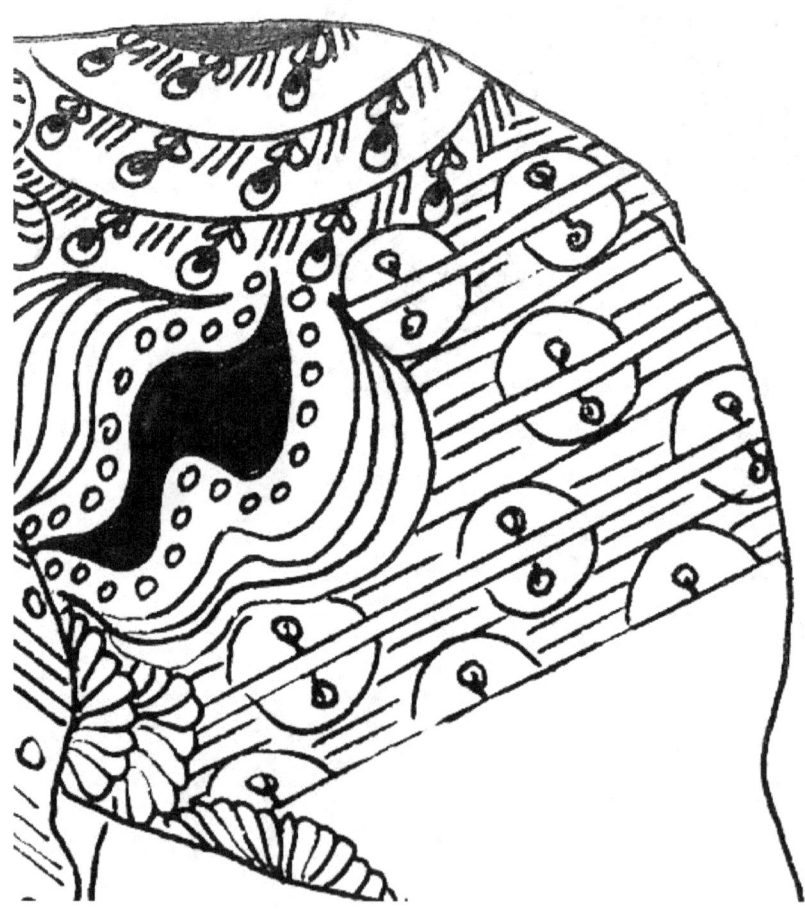

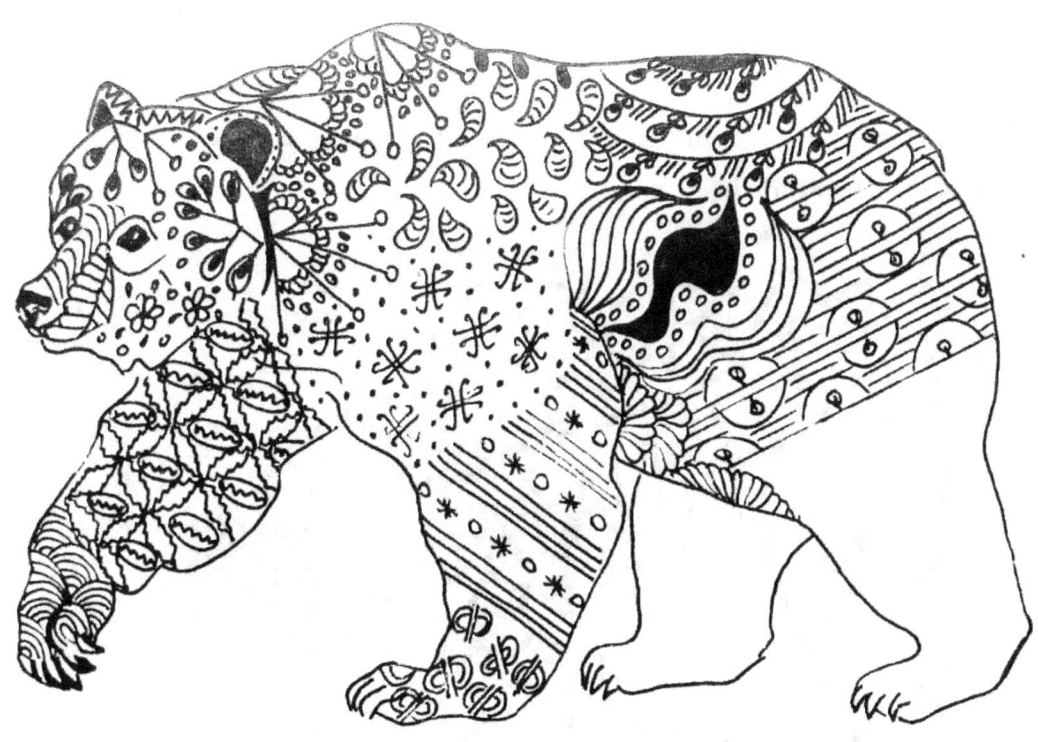

Step 9

Keeping the abbly pattern in mind, draw a similar design in the hind leg and draw a few arcs around the flowers.

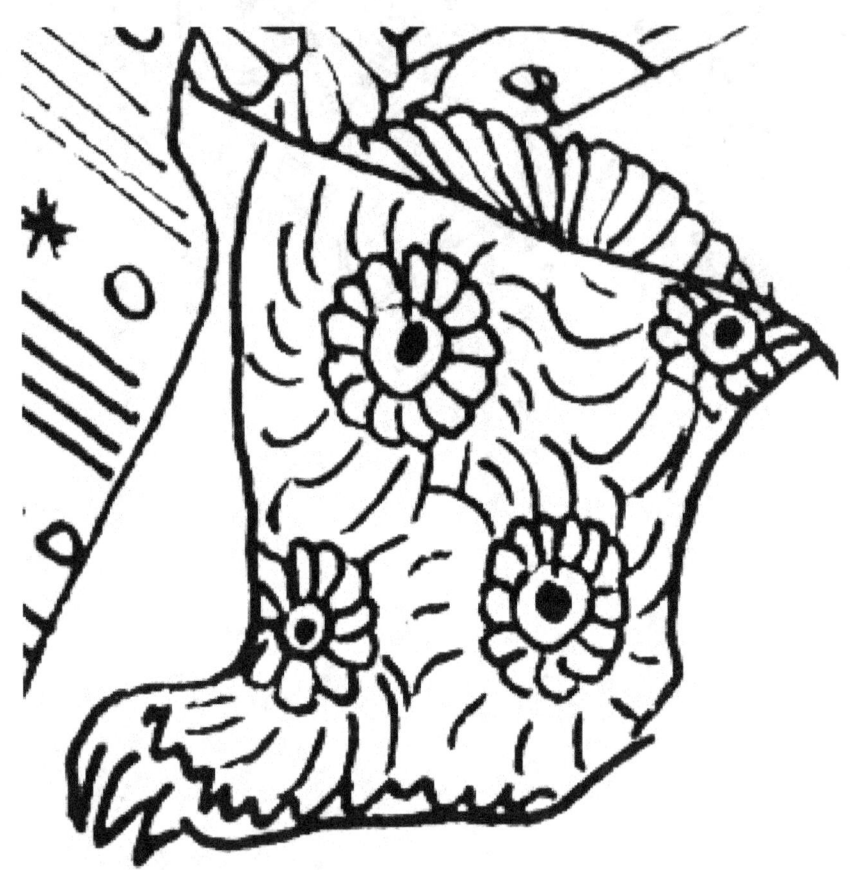

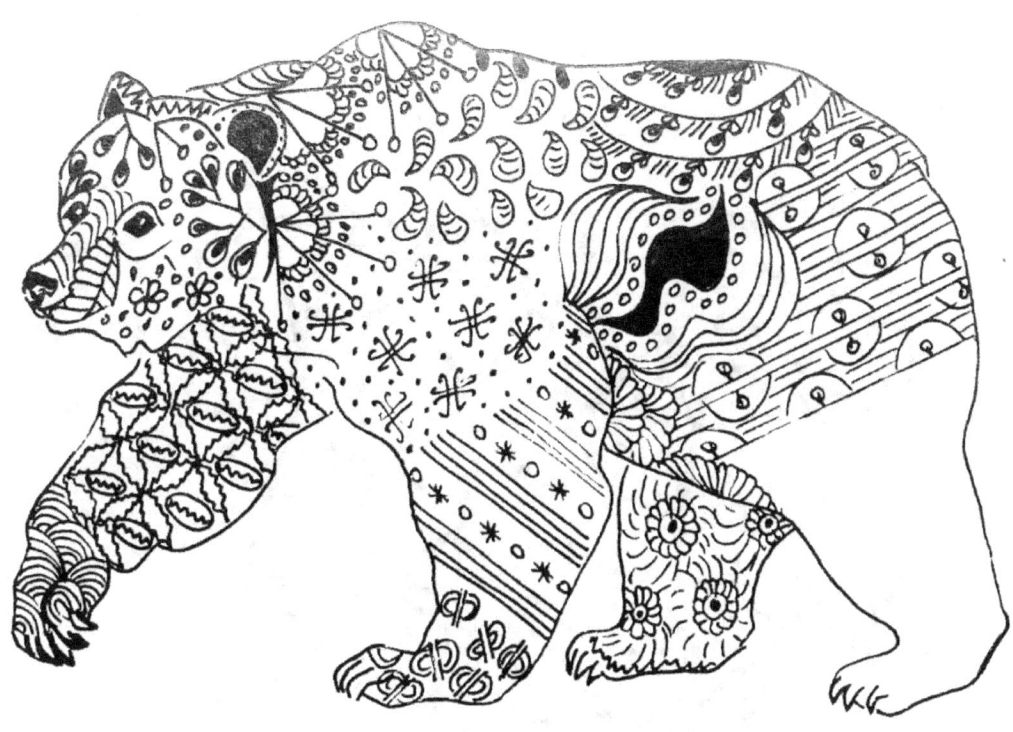

Step 10

Fill up the hind leg of the bear with difky pattern.

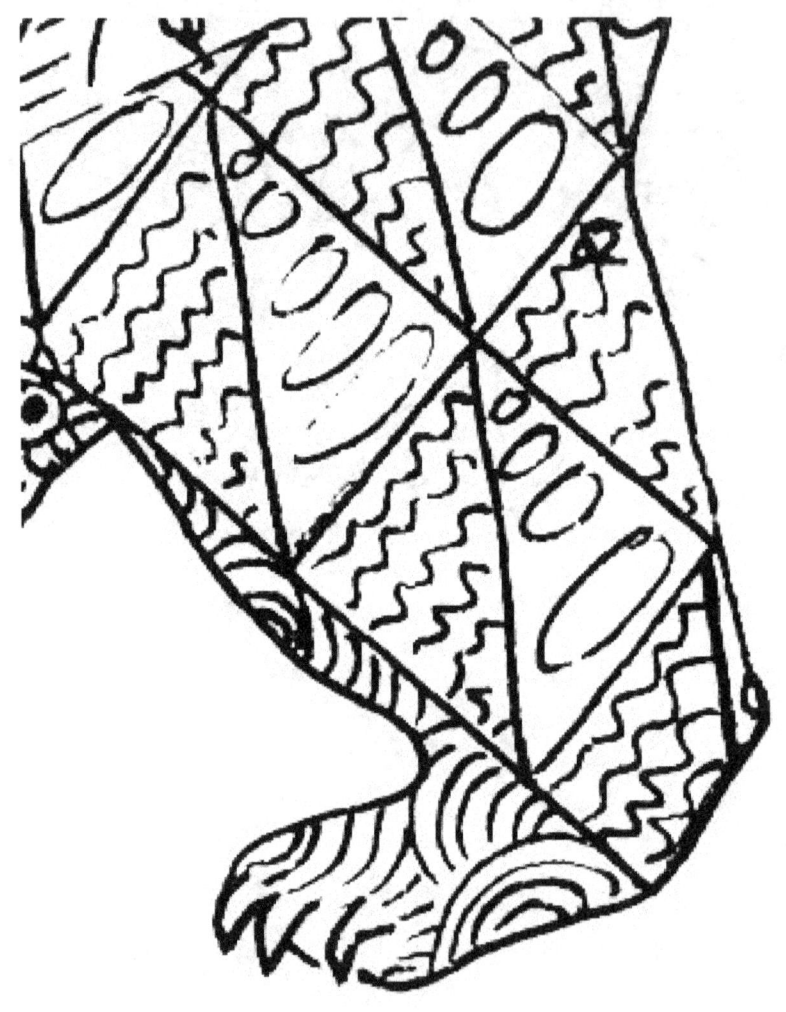

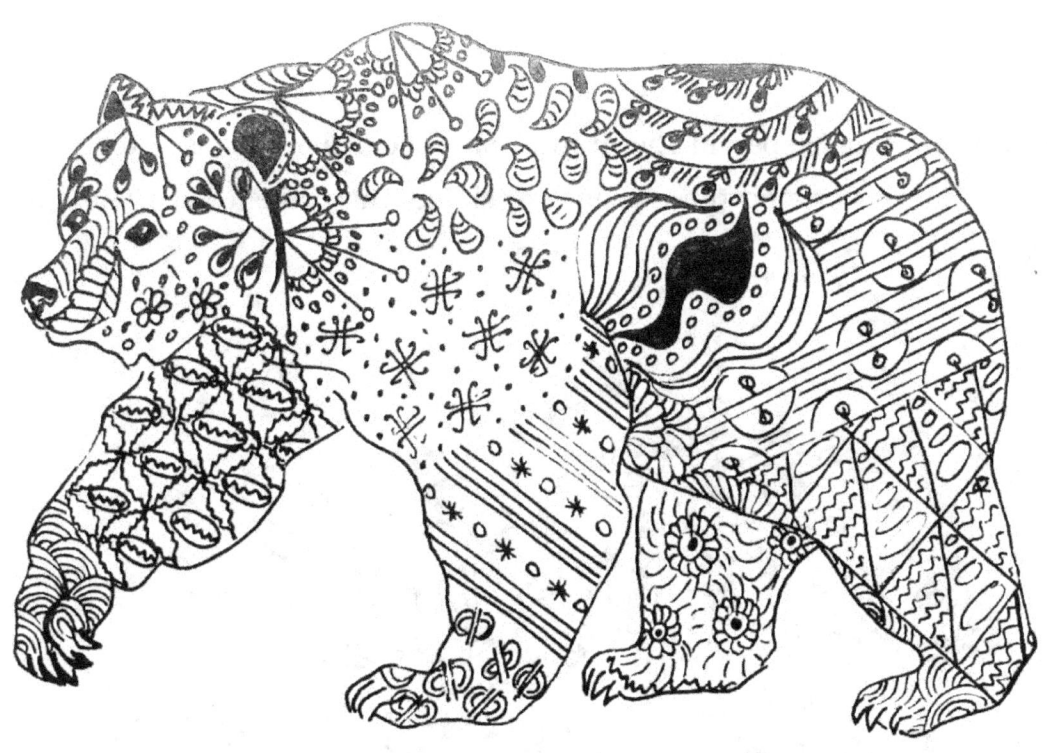

Step 11

Draw a few star shapes in the ground on which, the bear is walking and draw a few arcs around these shapes to signify the presence of ground and mud.

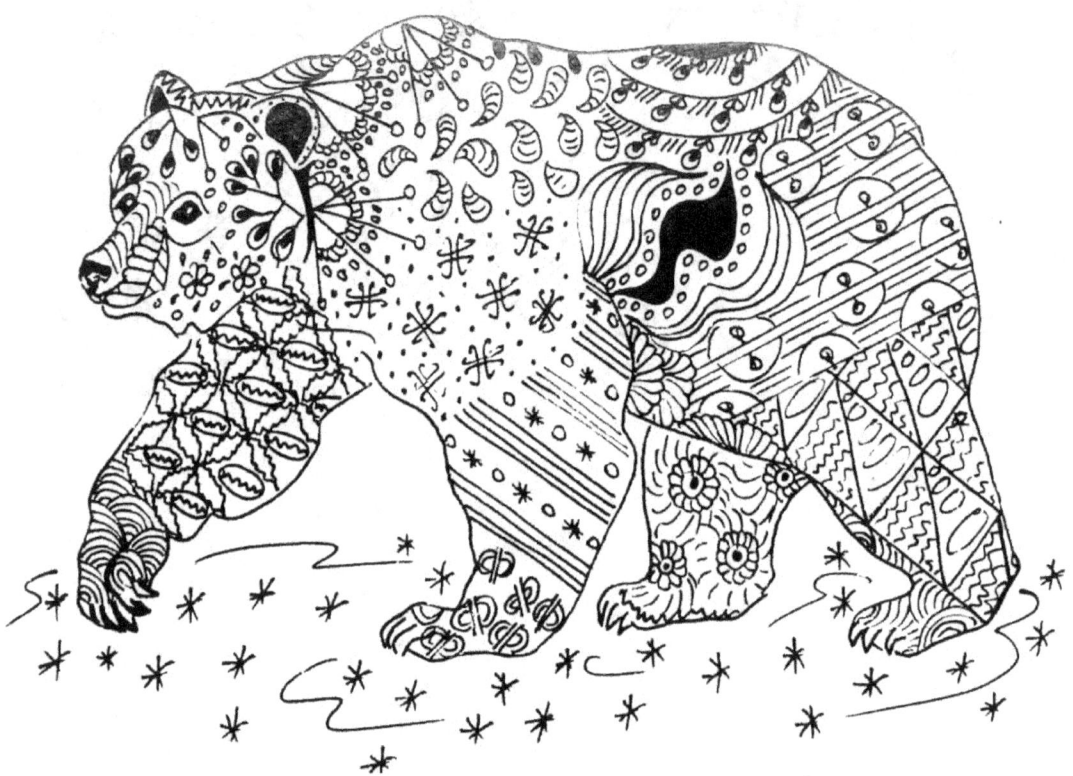

Drawing 2
Elephant

Step 1

Draw the basic outline of an elephant, of which, only three legs are visible.

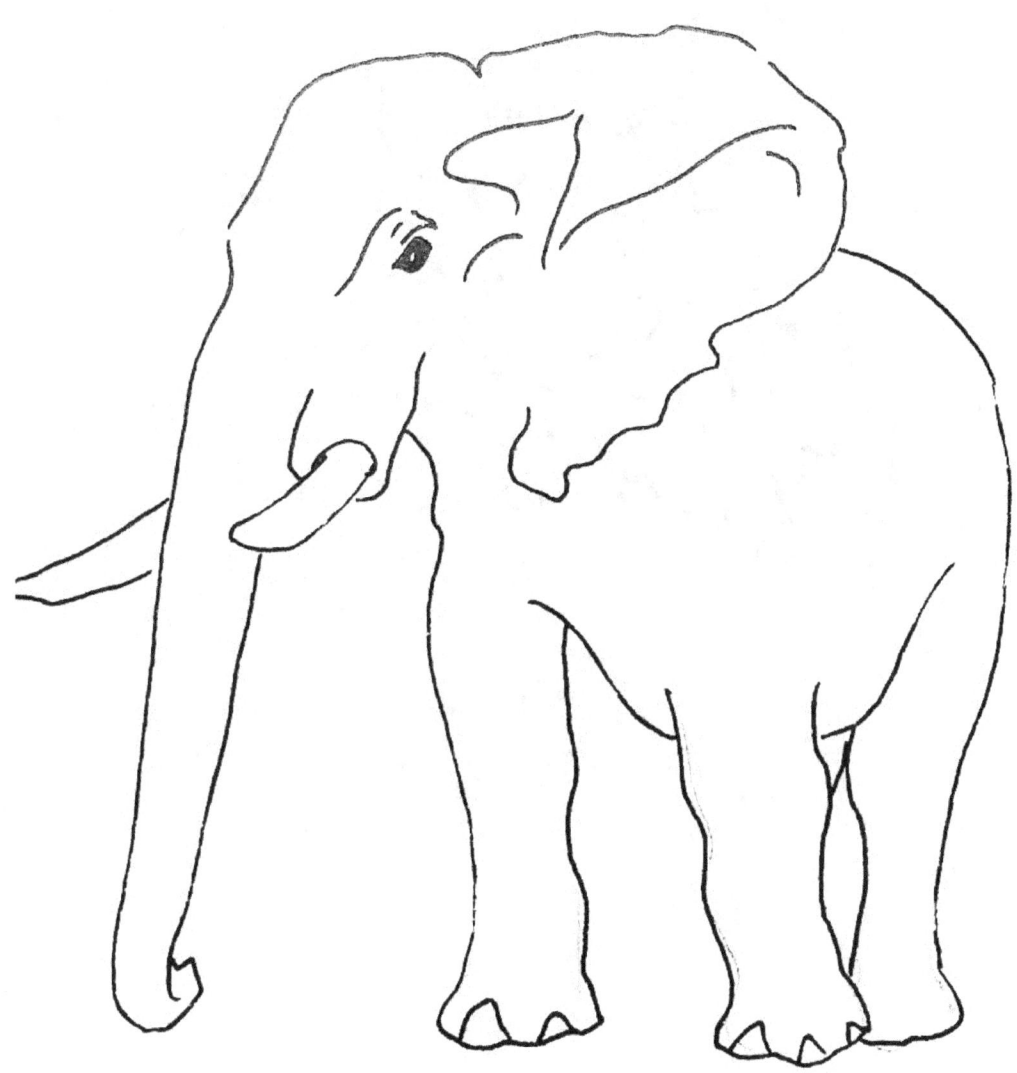

Step 2

Draw a few diamonds in the forehead of the elephant and connect them with zigzag lines. You might have learnt this pattern in the previous version of this book.

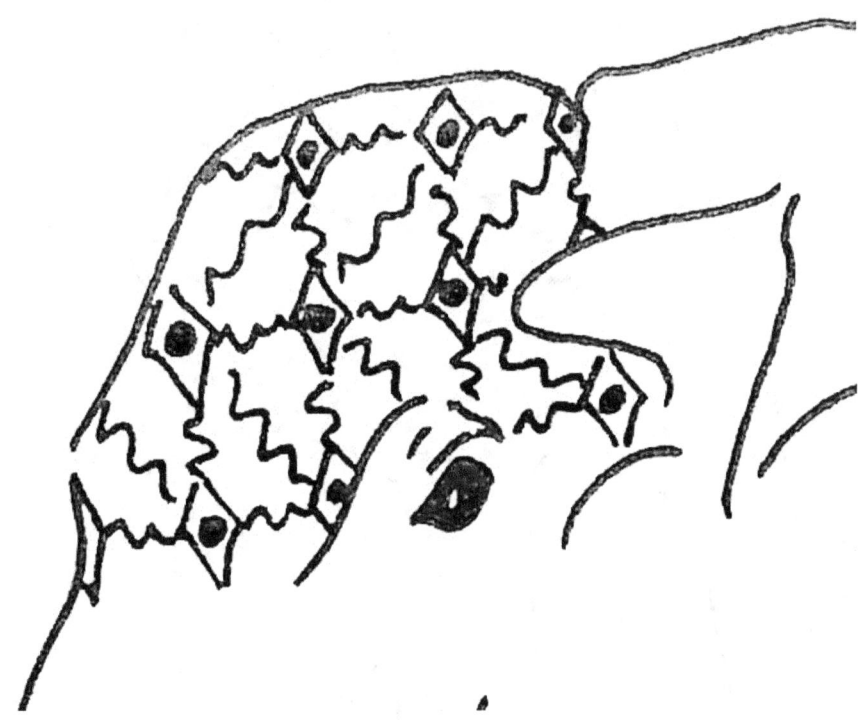

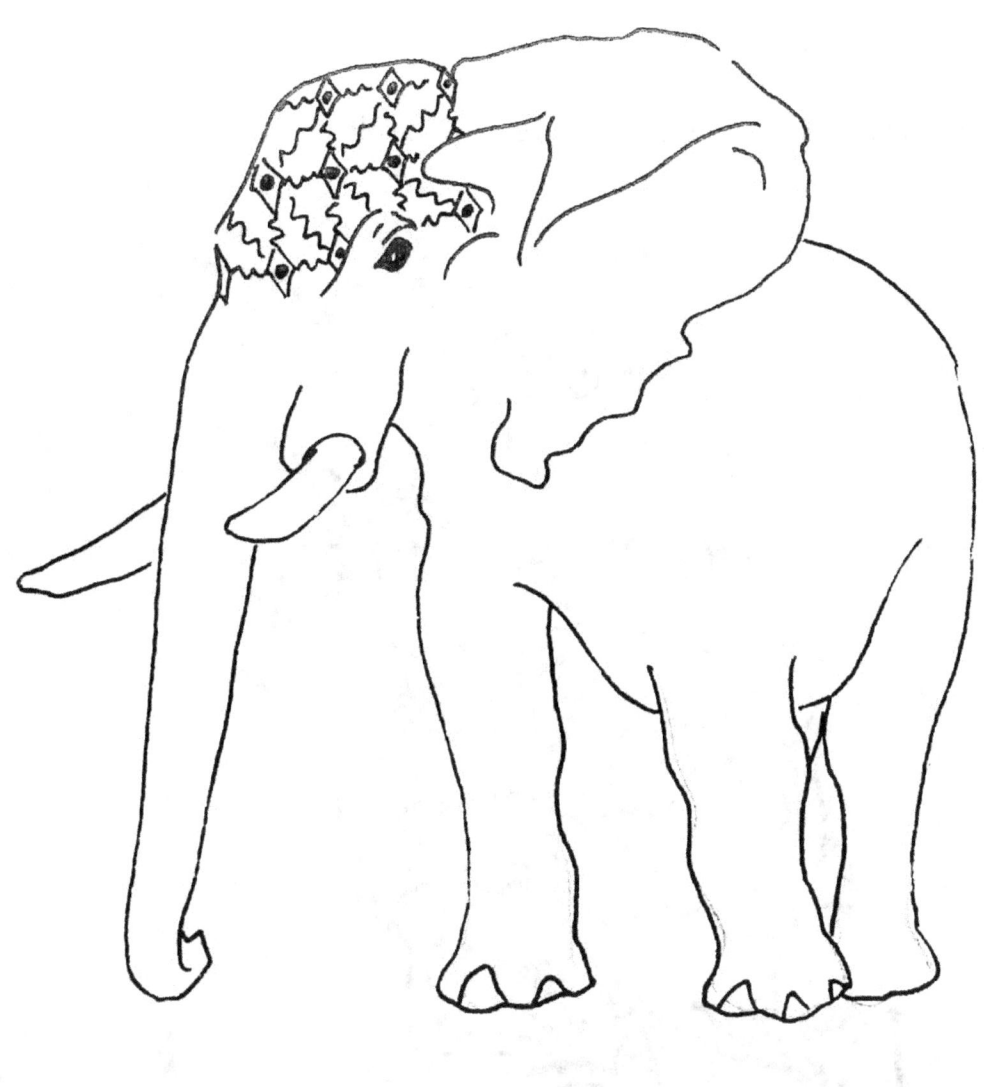

Step 3

Draw a few sets of scallops below the eye of the elephant.

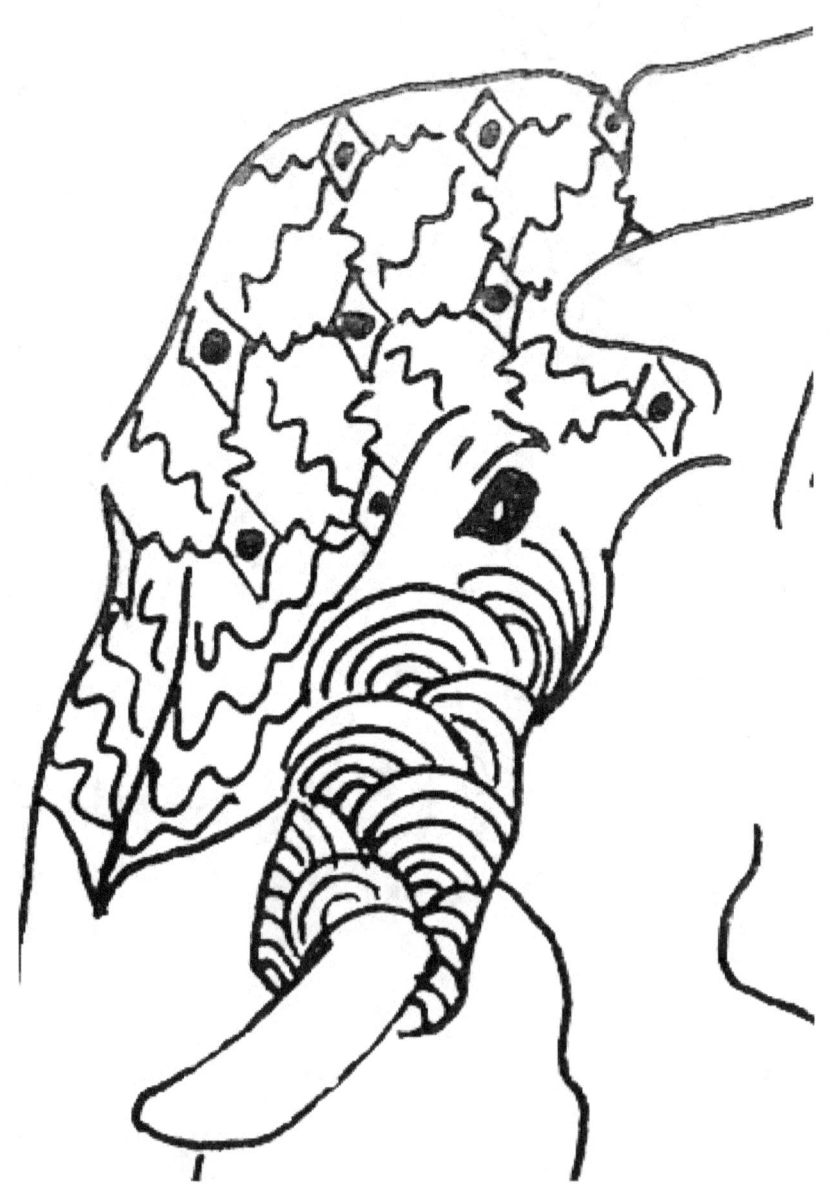

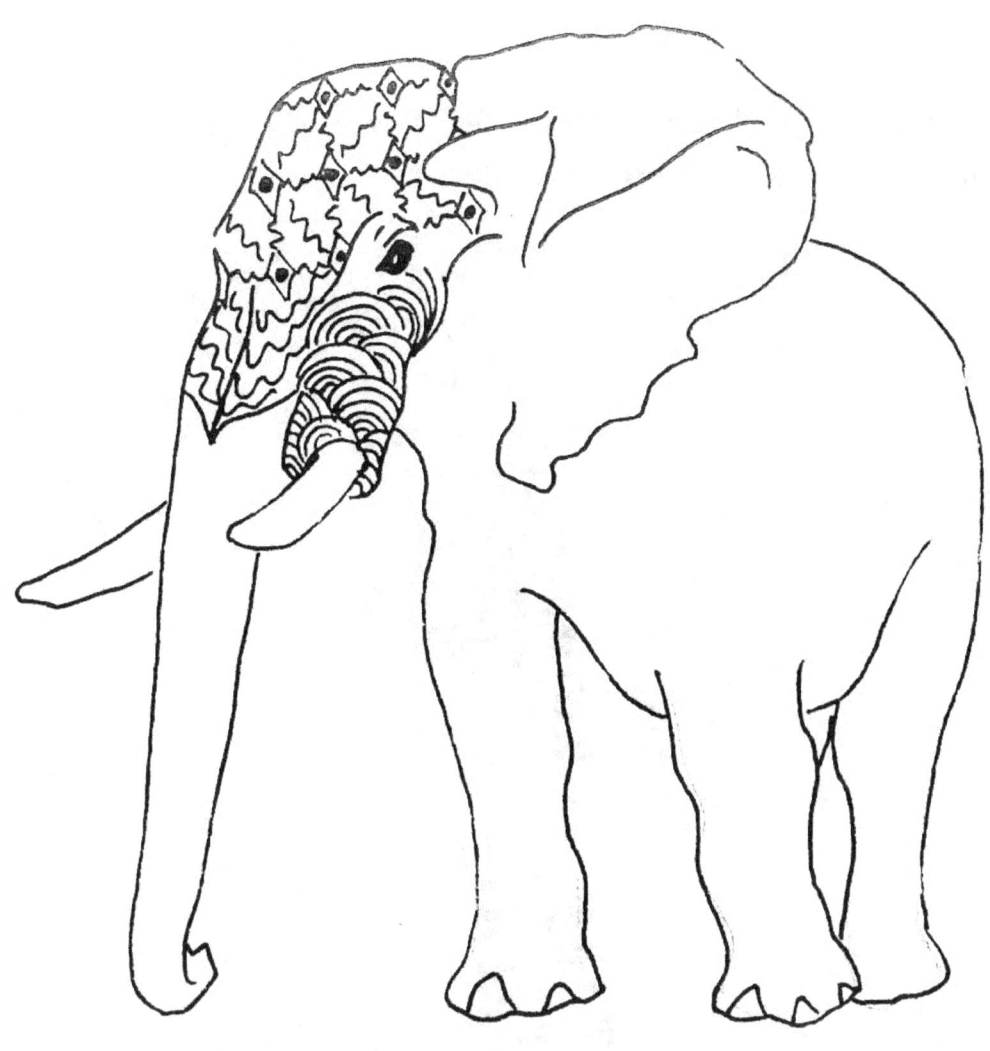

Step 4

In the trunk of the elephant, draw a few designs such as circles, waves, running stitches, and thick lines filled with ink.

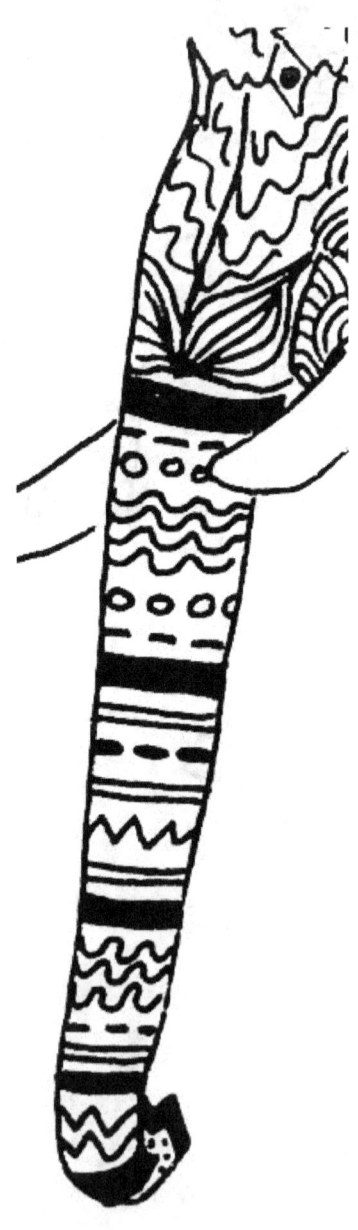

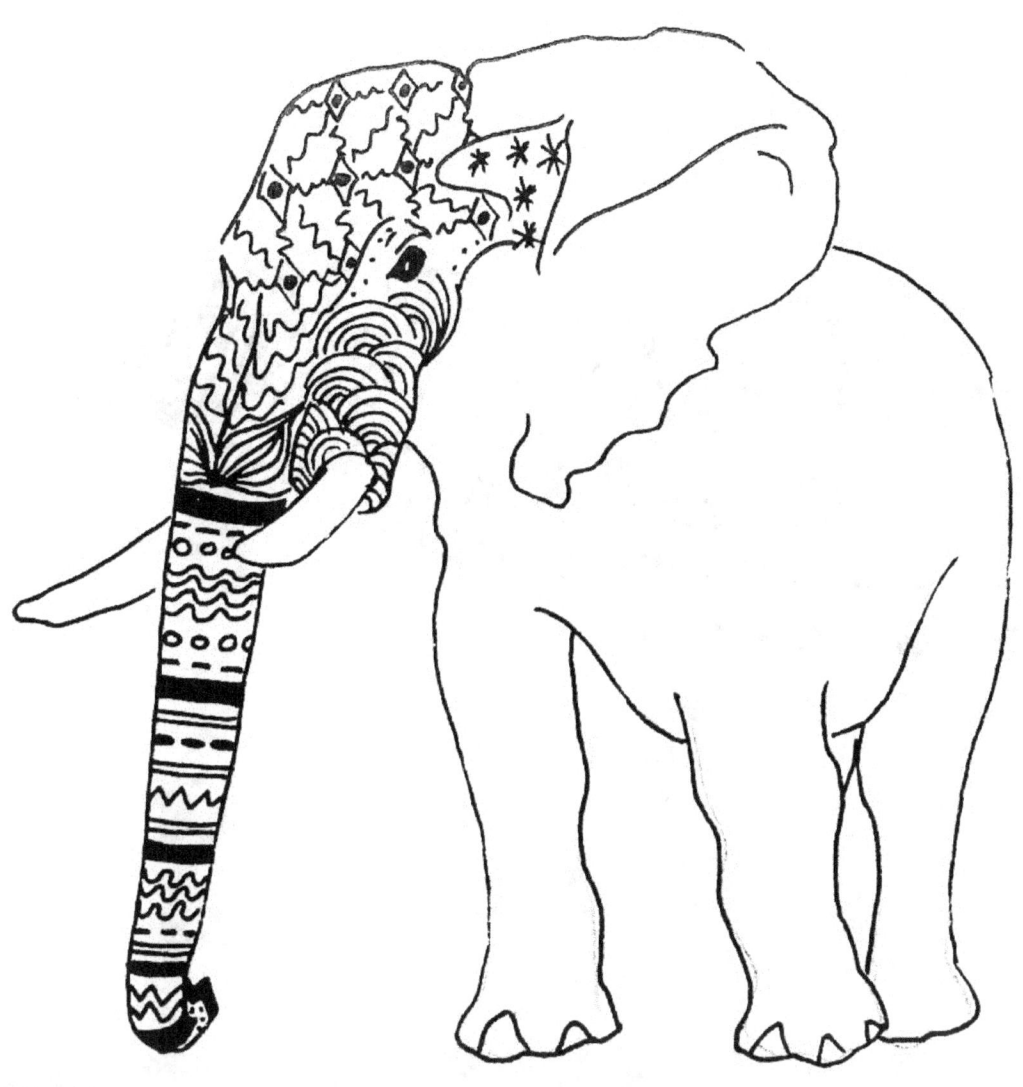

Step 5

Draw the beu pattern in the ear of the elephant.

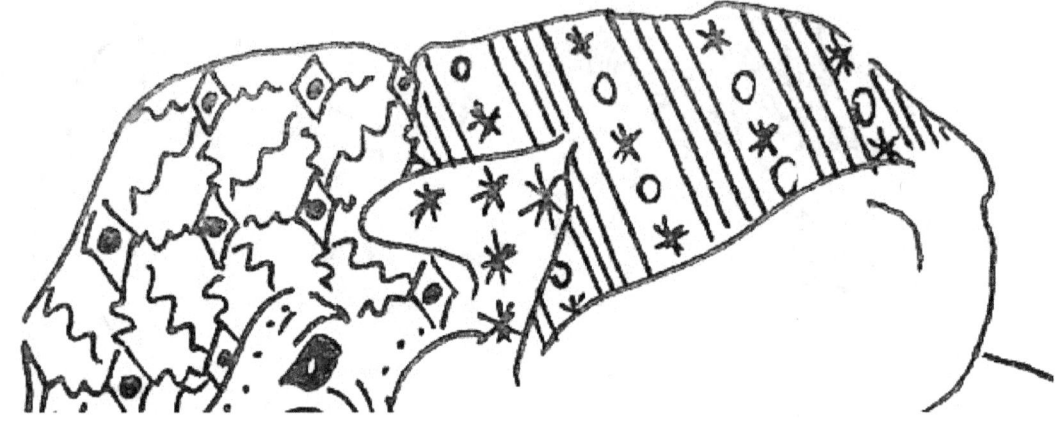

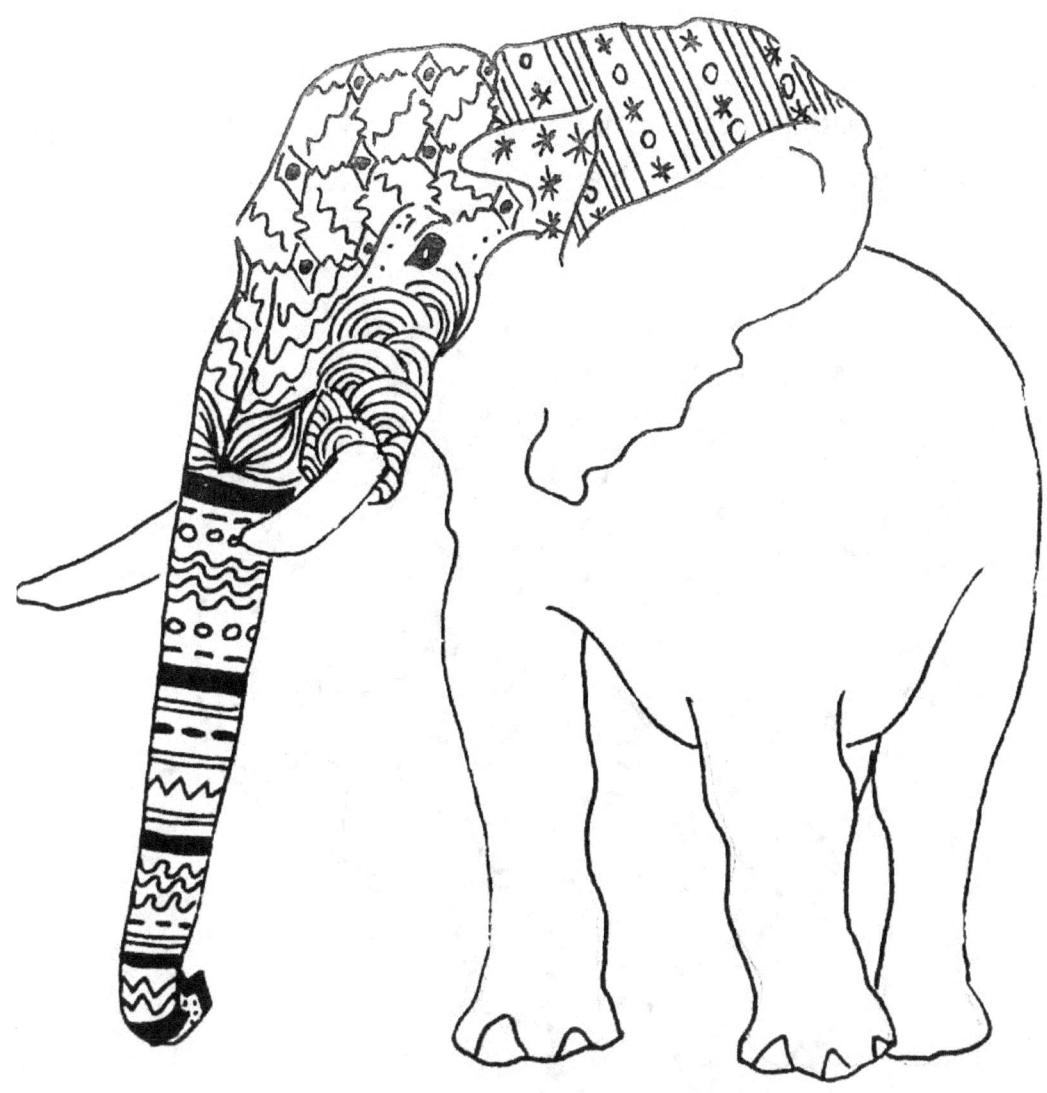

Step 6

Draw the calcy pattern in the remaining portion of the ear and highlight the outline of the ear with thick outline.

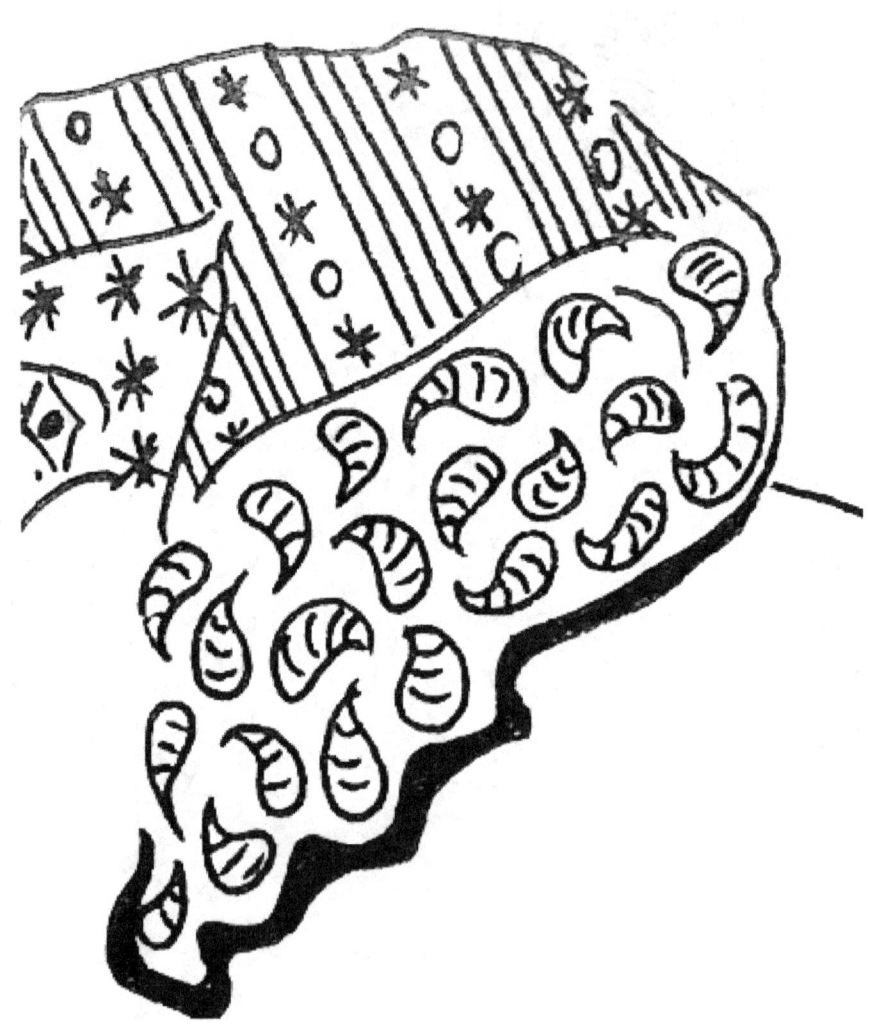

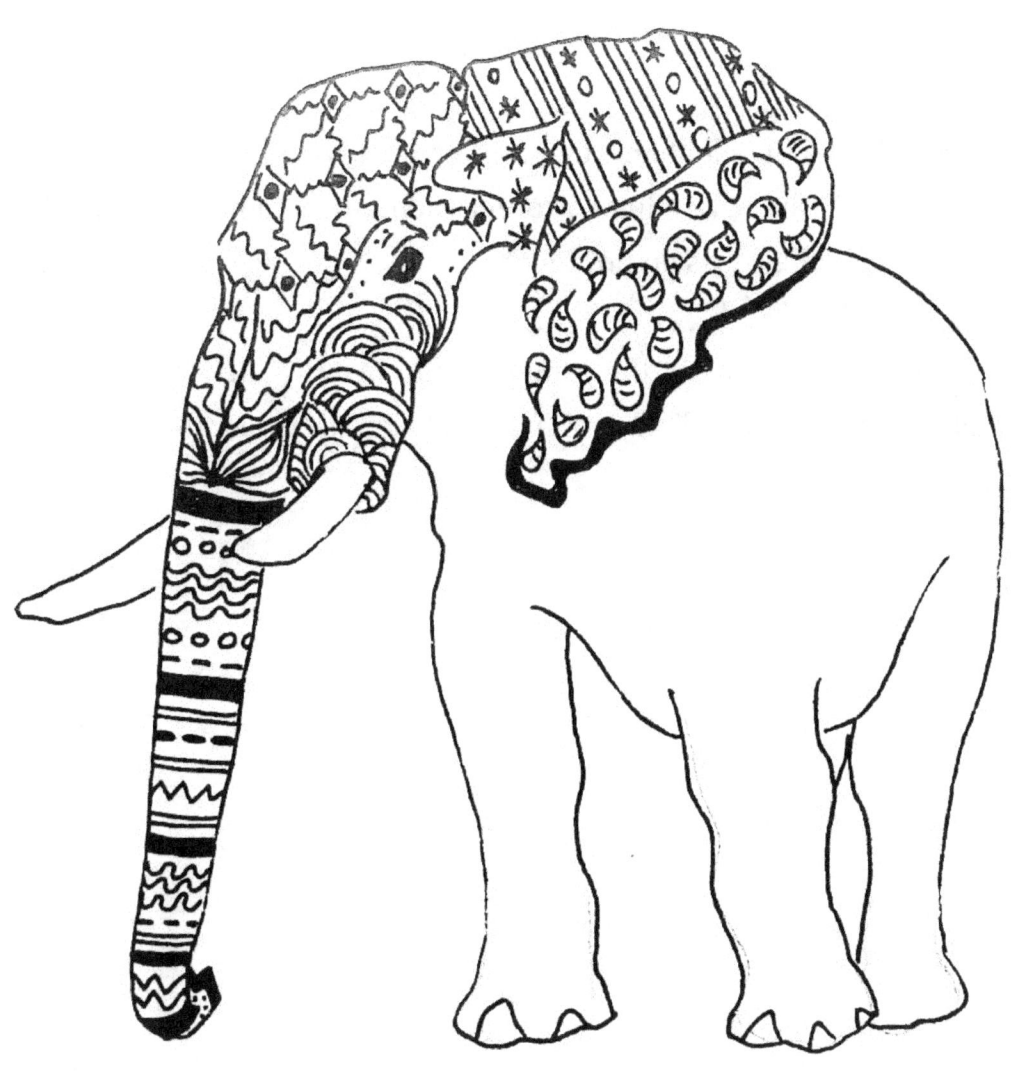

Step 7

In the front leg of the elephant, draw a few circles and encircle them with another circle. Draw a few lines around them such that they look like a square, of which, the edges do not touch.

Draw a few parallel lines in the same leg and insert a zigzag line between them. Now draw a perpendicular tree like pattern on the parallel lines.

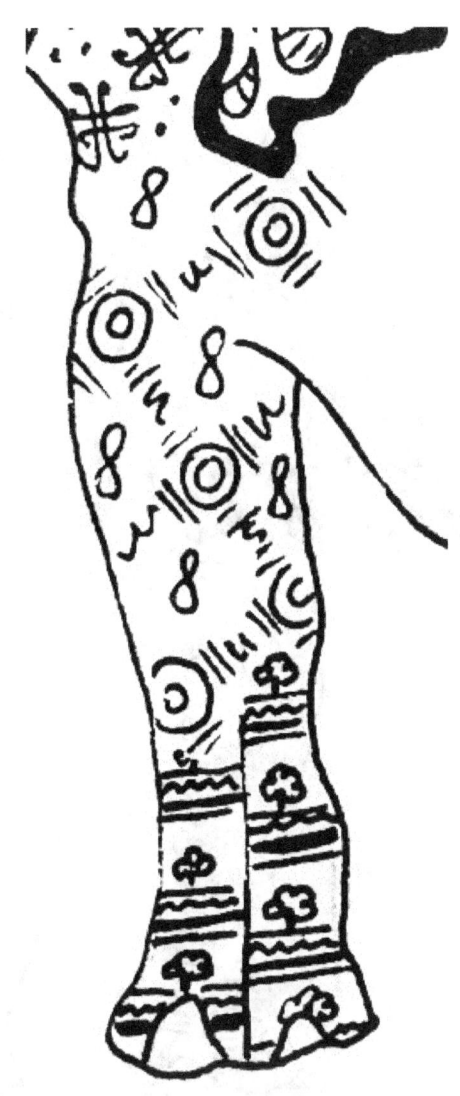

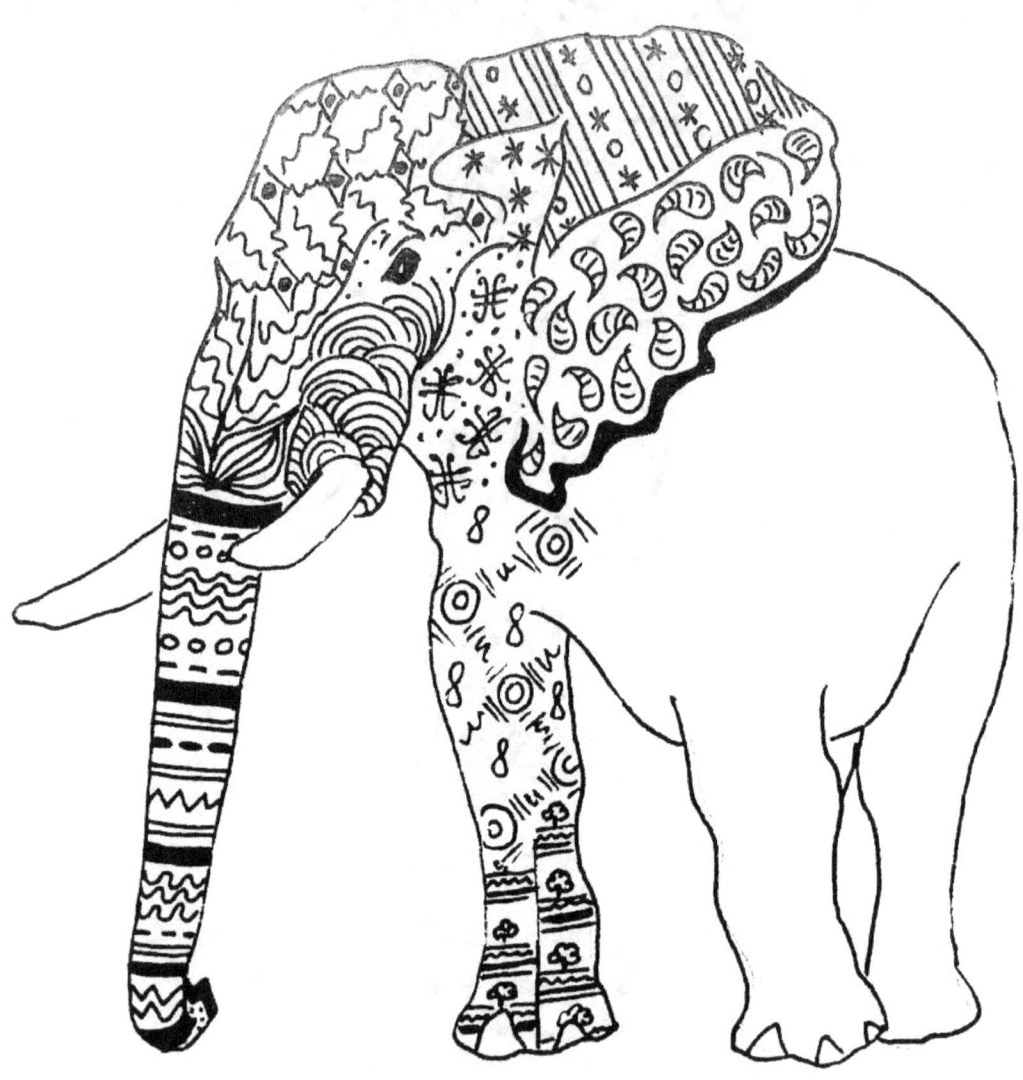

Step 8

Draw a few large waves in the back of the elephant and draw a few drops around the waves. Fill the alternate set of drops on the waves with ink.

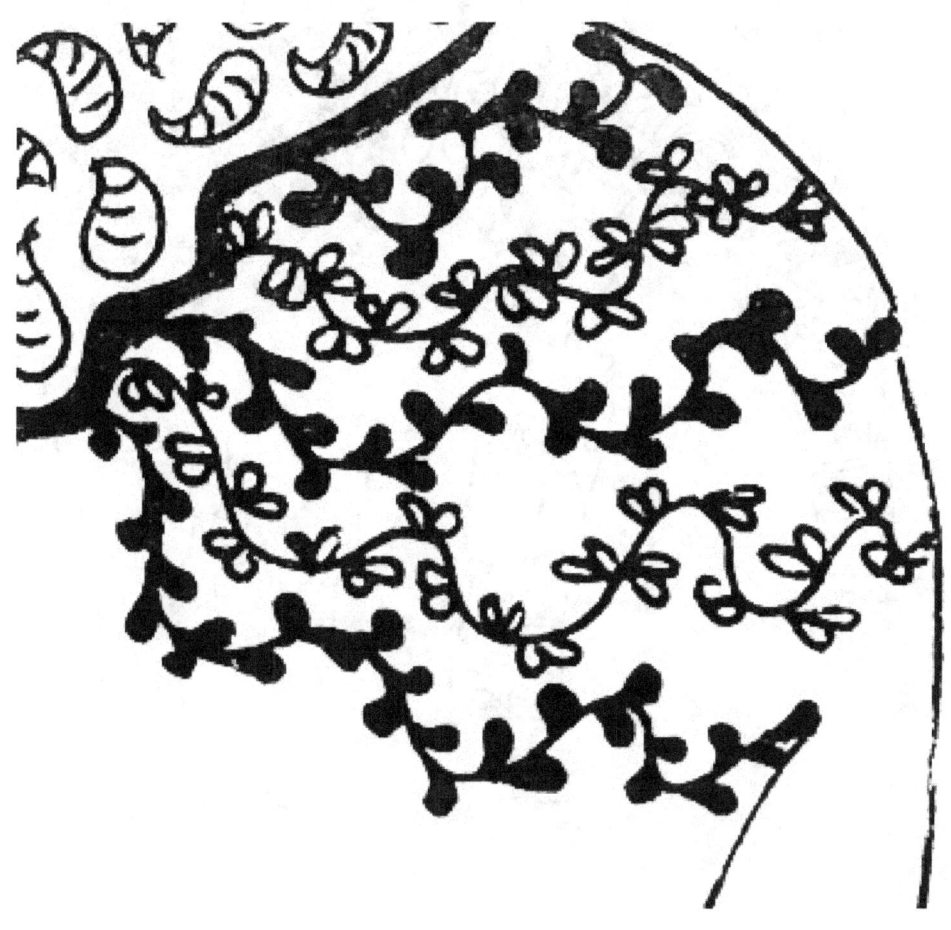

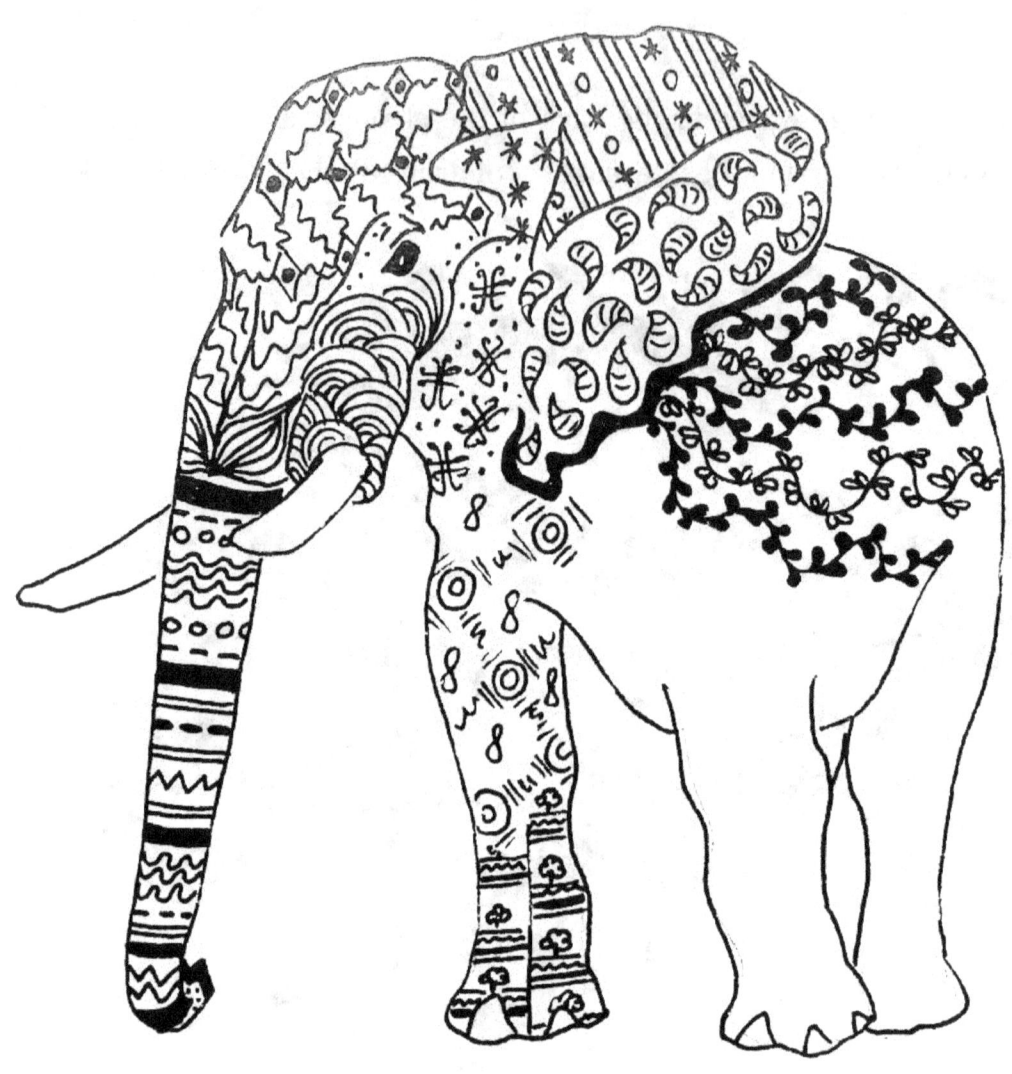

Step 9

Draw the norl pattern above the back leg. Divide one of the hind legs into a few triangles and draw a few flowers in the triangles. In the other hind leg, draw a few large circles and draw a smaller circle in its center. Draw a few arcs emerging from the center of the smaller circle. In the remaining portion of the leg, draw a few discs and fill the alternate set of discs with ink. Draw a few lines in the remaining set of discs as shown in the picture.

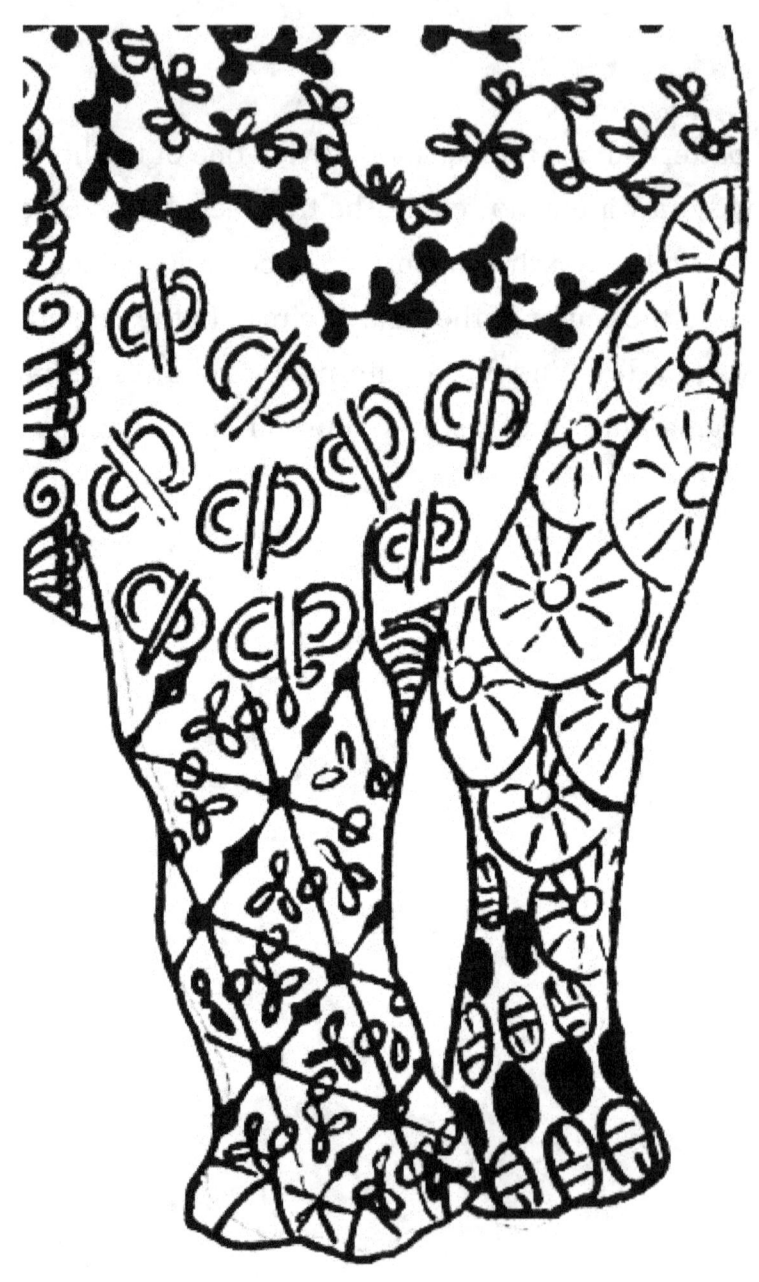

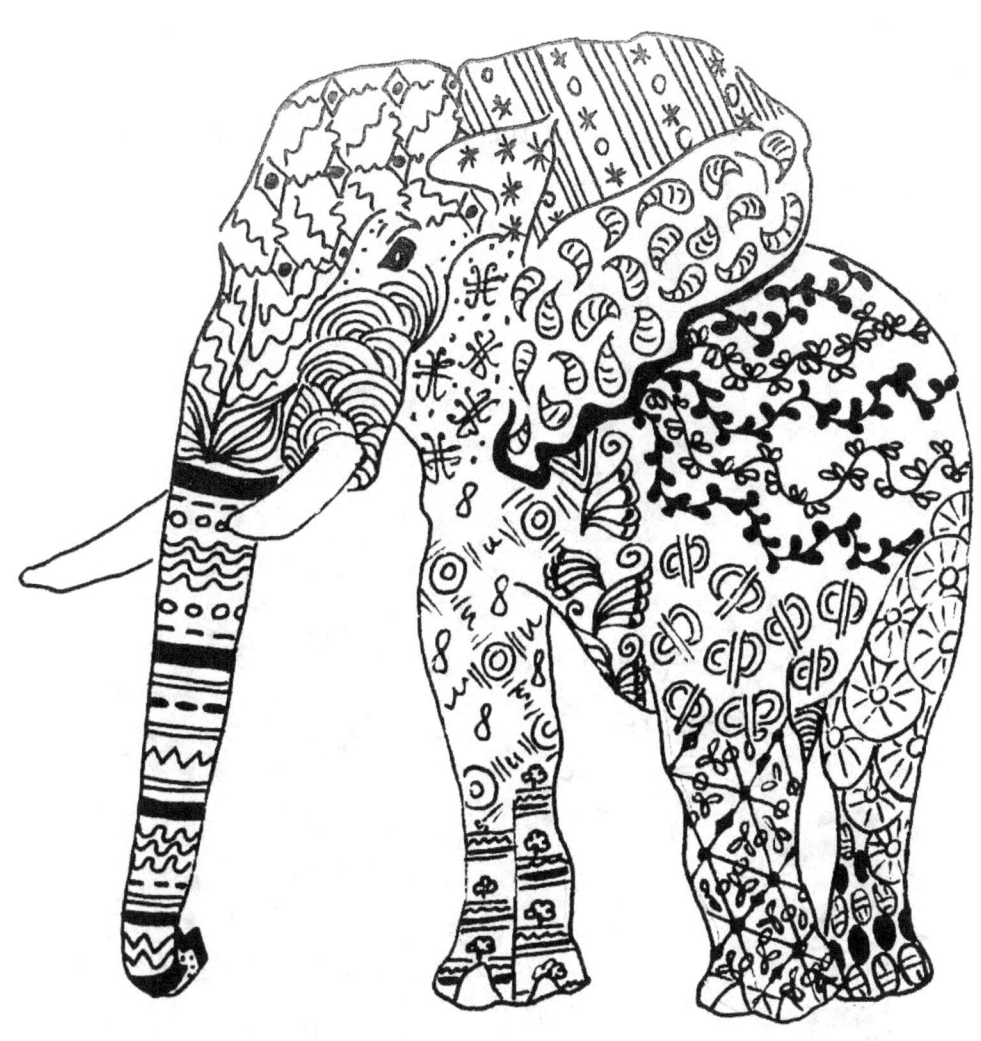

Step 10

Draw a few drops of water around the feet and trunk of the elephant as shown in the illustration.

The drawing of Zen Doodle elephant is complete.

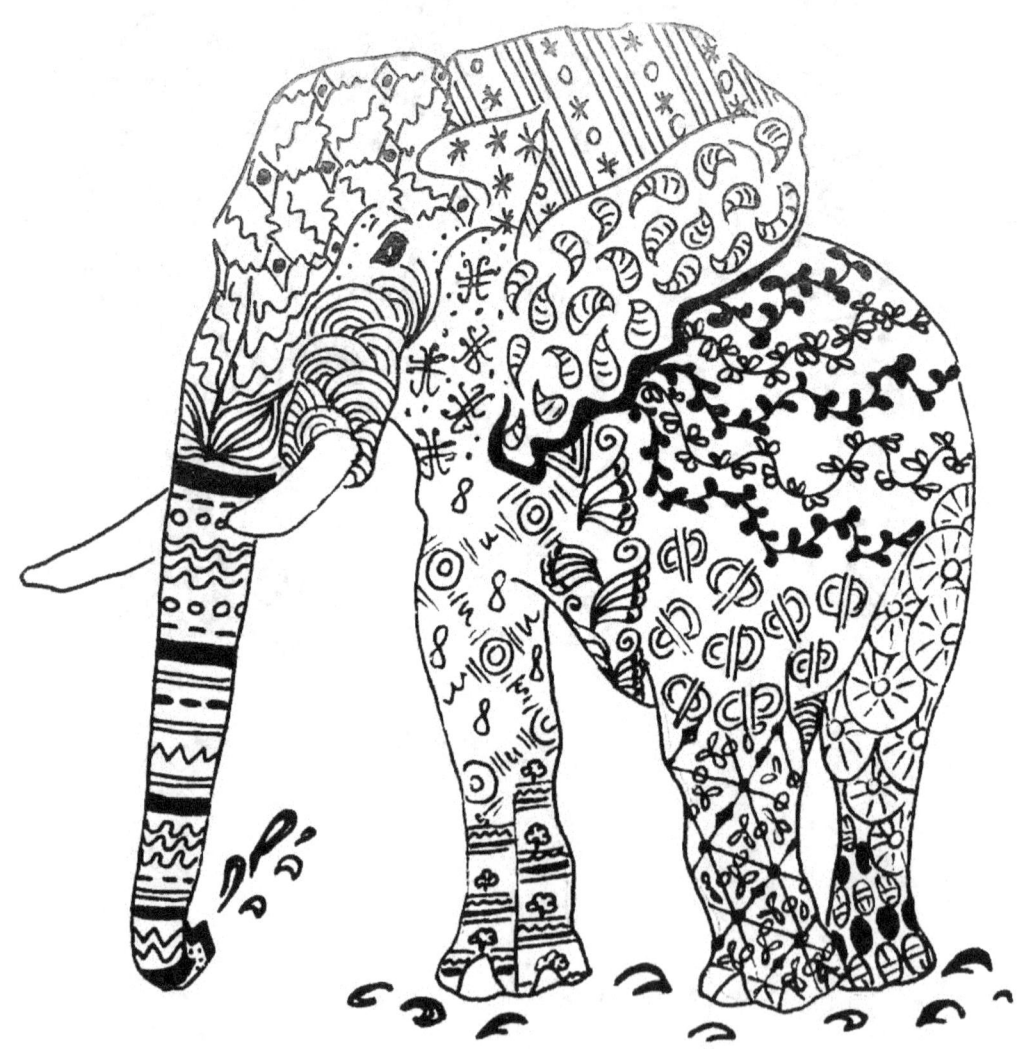

Drawing 3
Flowers

Draw the outline of a few flowers in the middle of a drawing sheet.

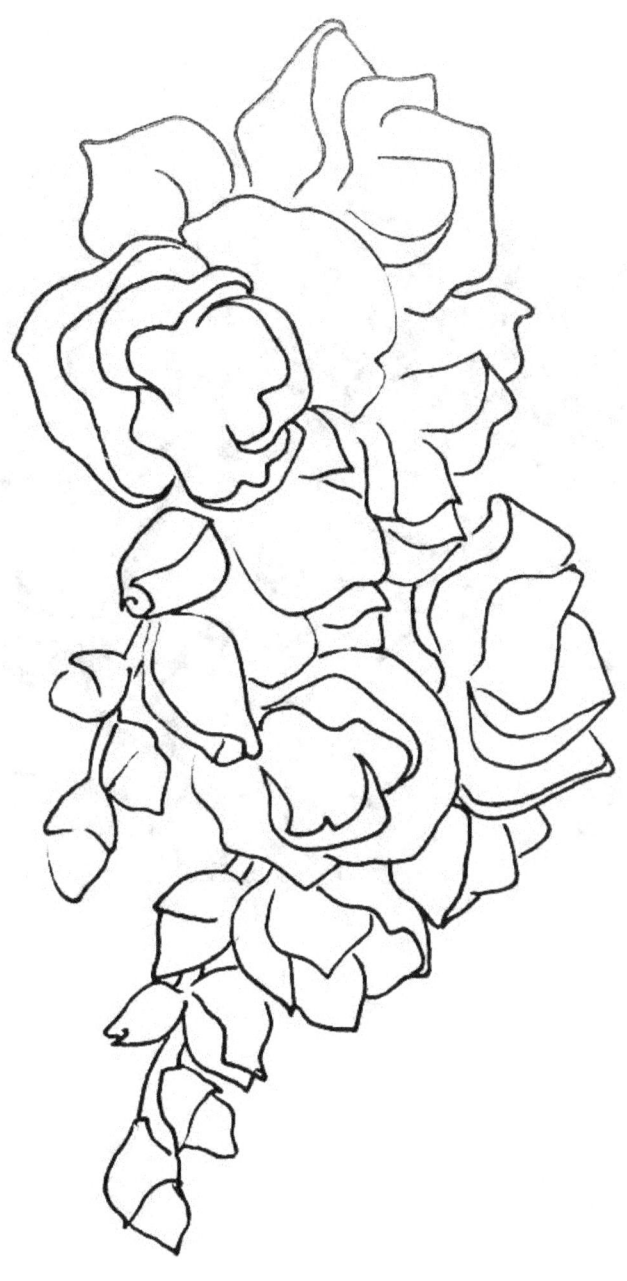

Step 2

Draw a negative zigzag pattern in one of the petals. Take a few petals and draw patterns in them such as vertical lines, flowers, zigzag lines, thick lines, circles, bullets, veins of flowers.

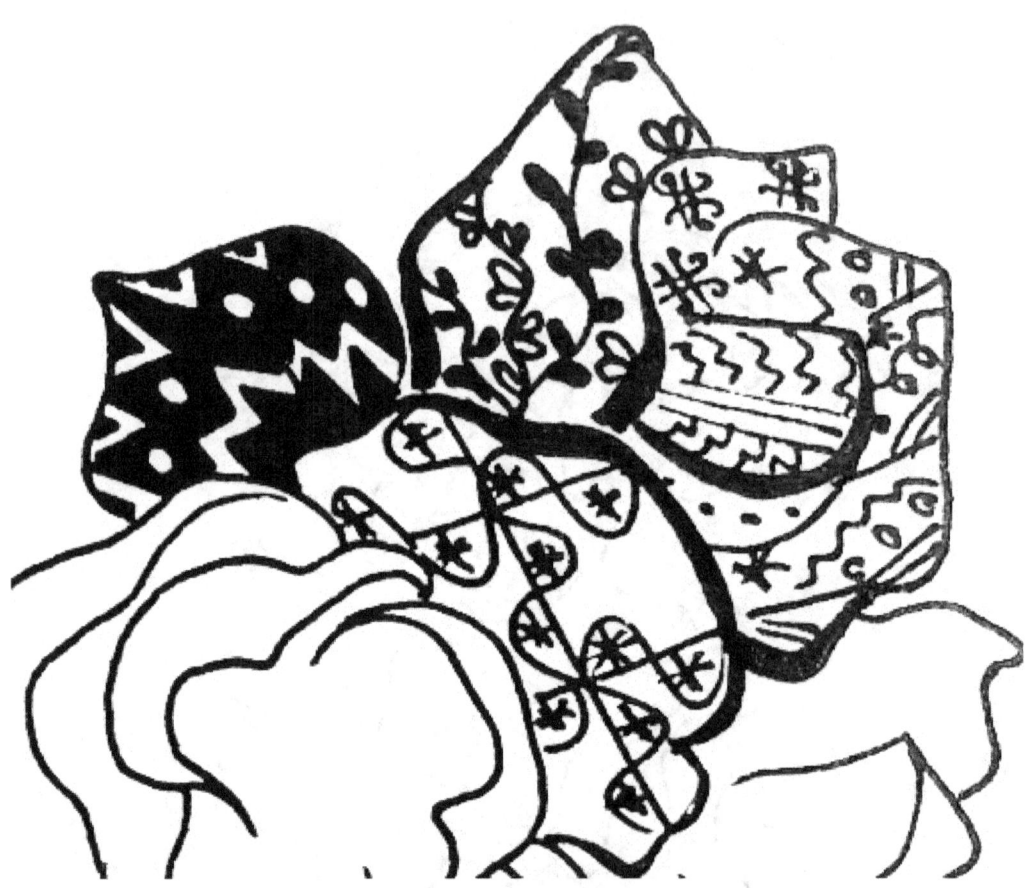

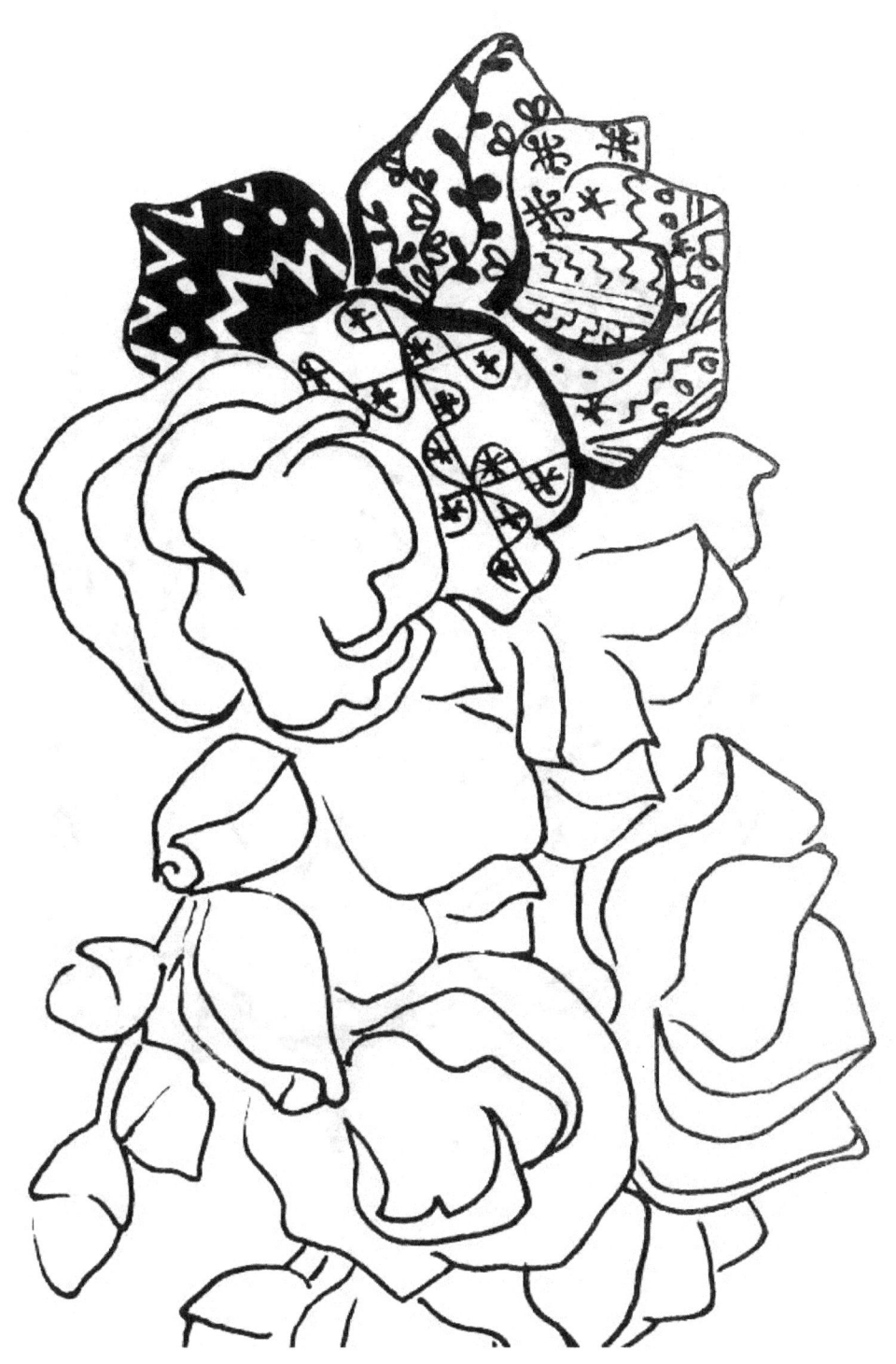

Step 3

Draw a few thick lines between the petals so that you can divide the chunks of petals into a small number of sections.

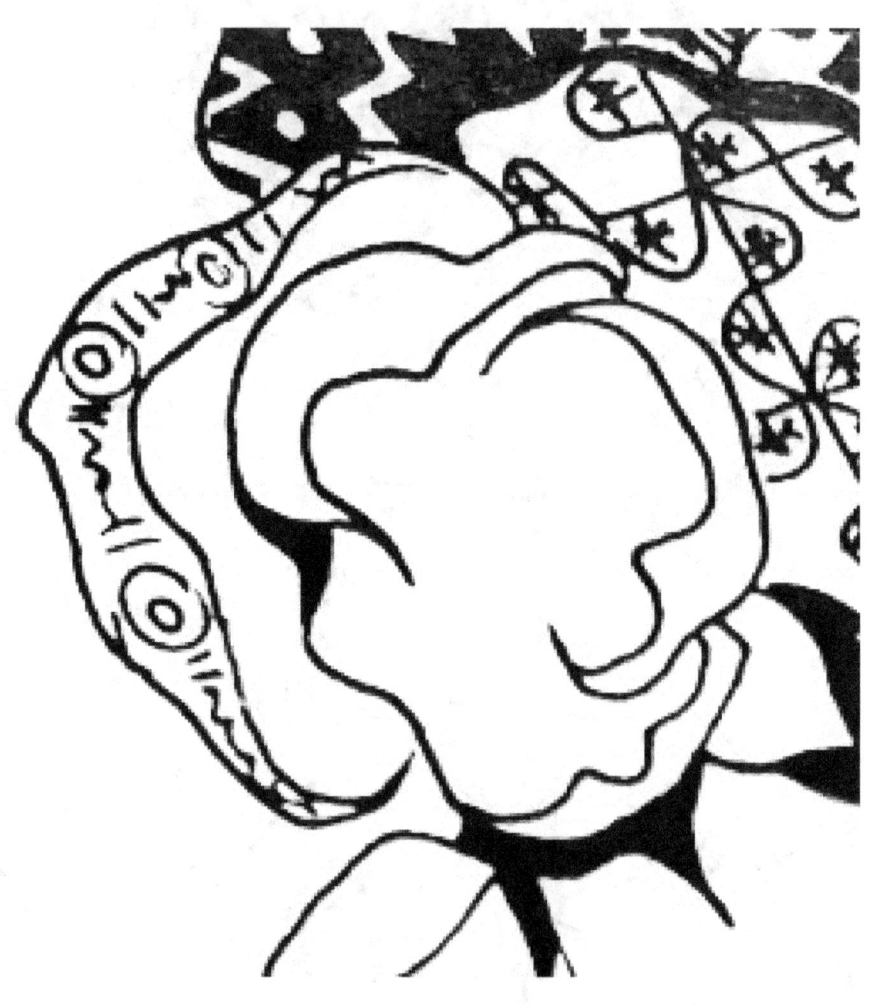

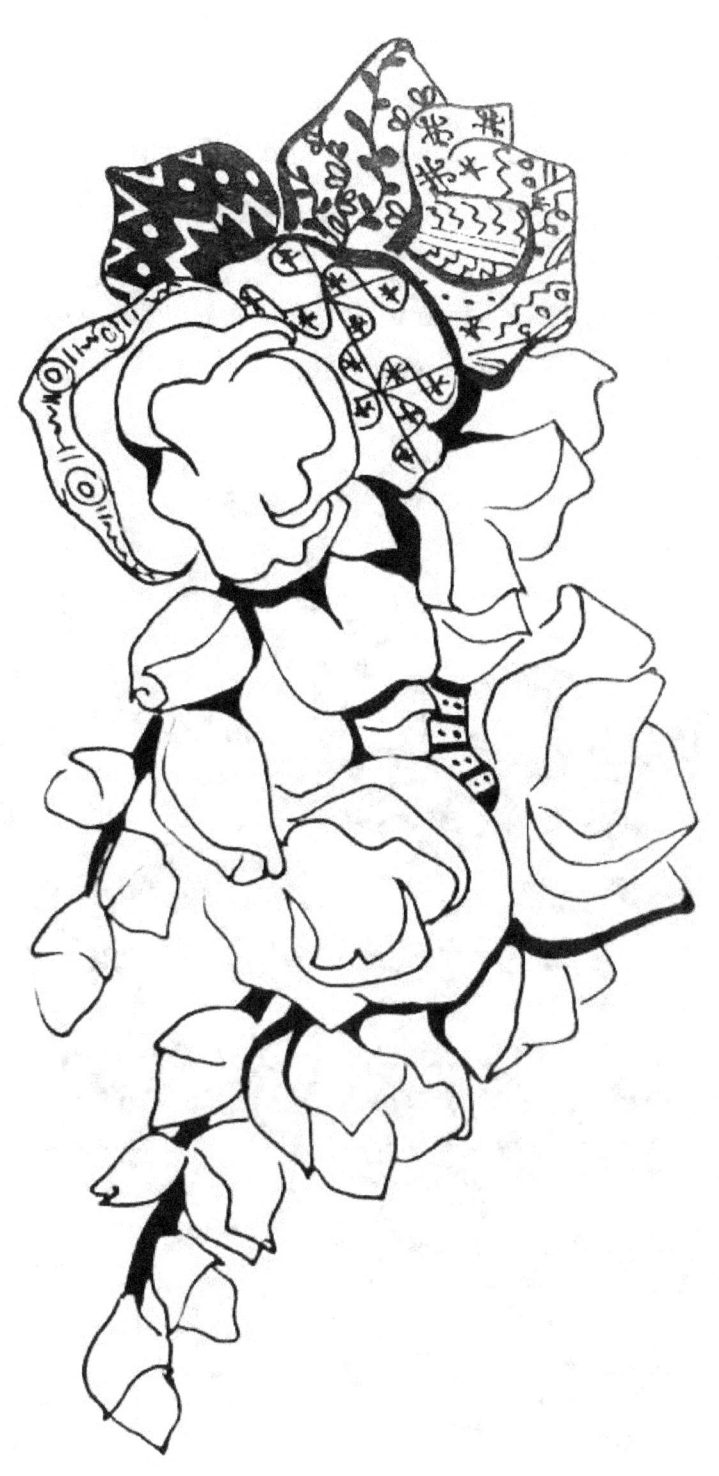

Step 4

Draw a few ovals in the one of the petals and fill them alternatively with ink. Draw a few vertical and horizontal lines perpendicular to each other in the remaining discs.

Draw a few concentric circles in one of the lower petals. Draw a few squares in the petals and surround them with waves.

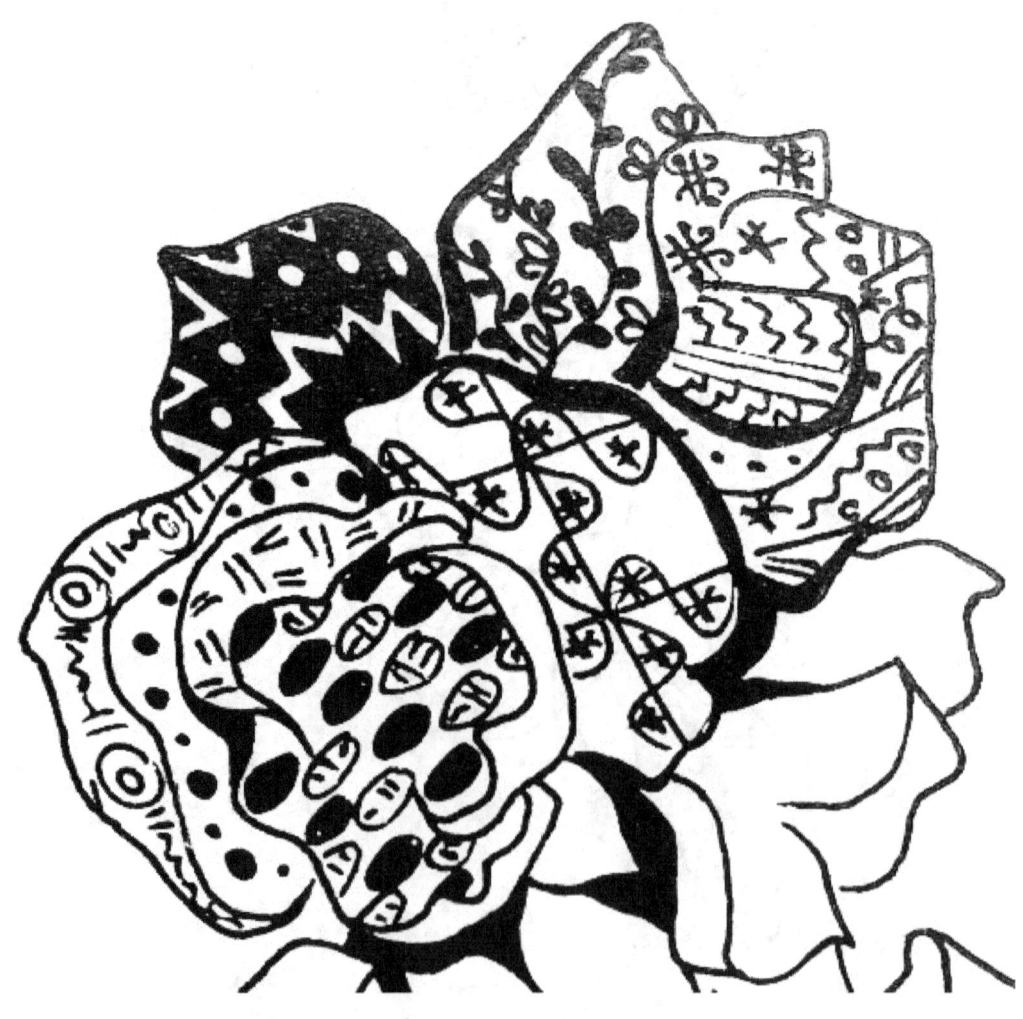

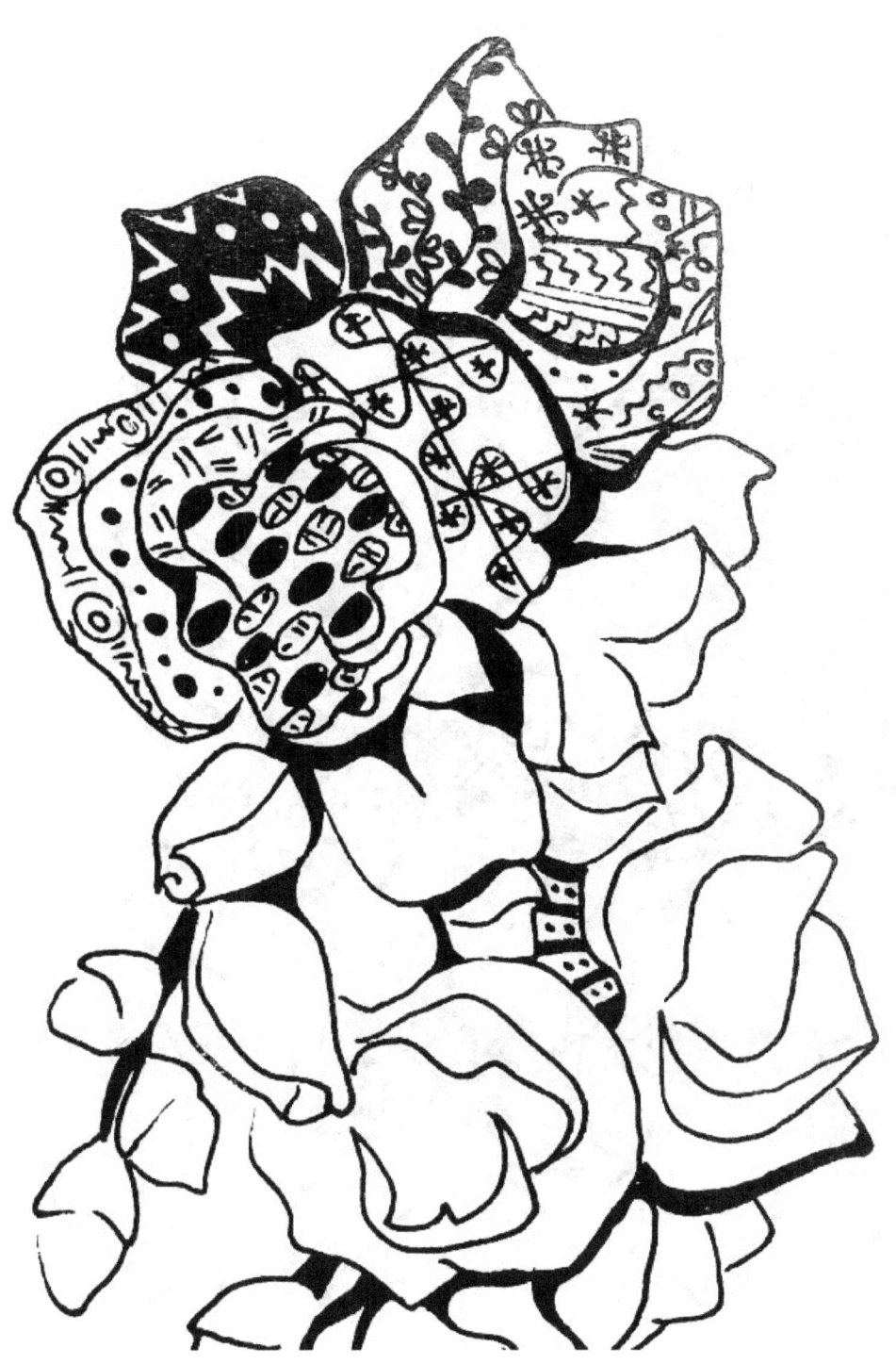

Step 5

Draw a few crossing lines in the middle portion of the flowers and surround them with dots. Draw a few patterns such as sets of scallop, thick parallel lines with dots between them, arcs, etc.

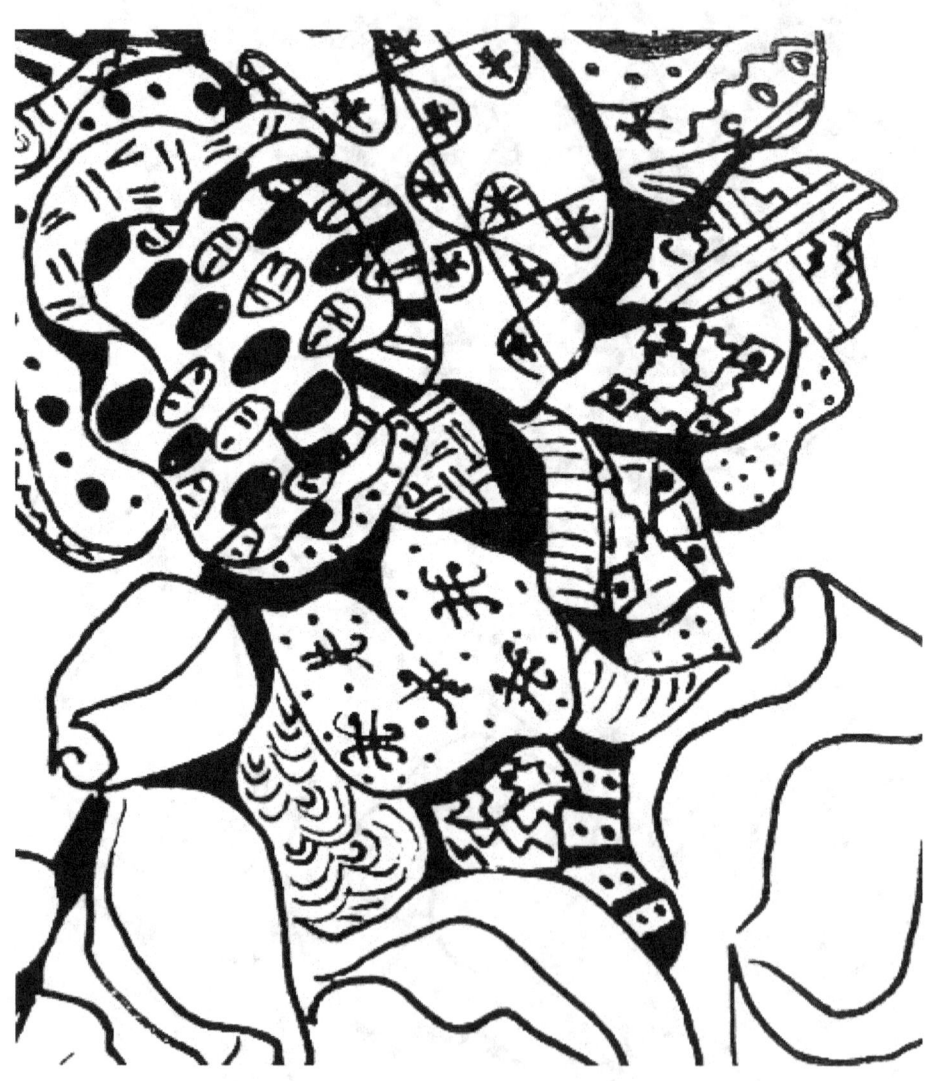

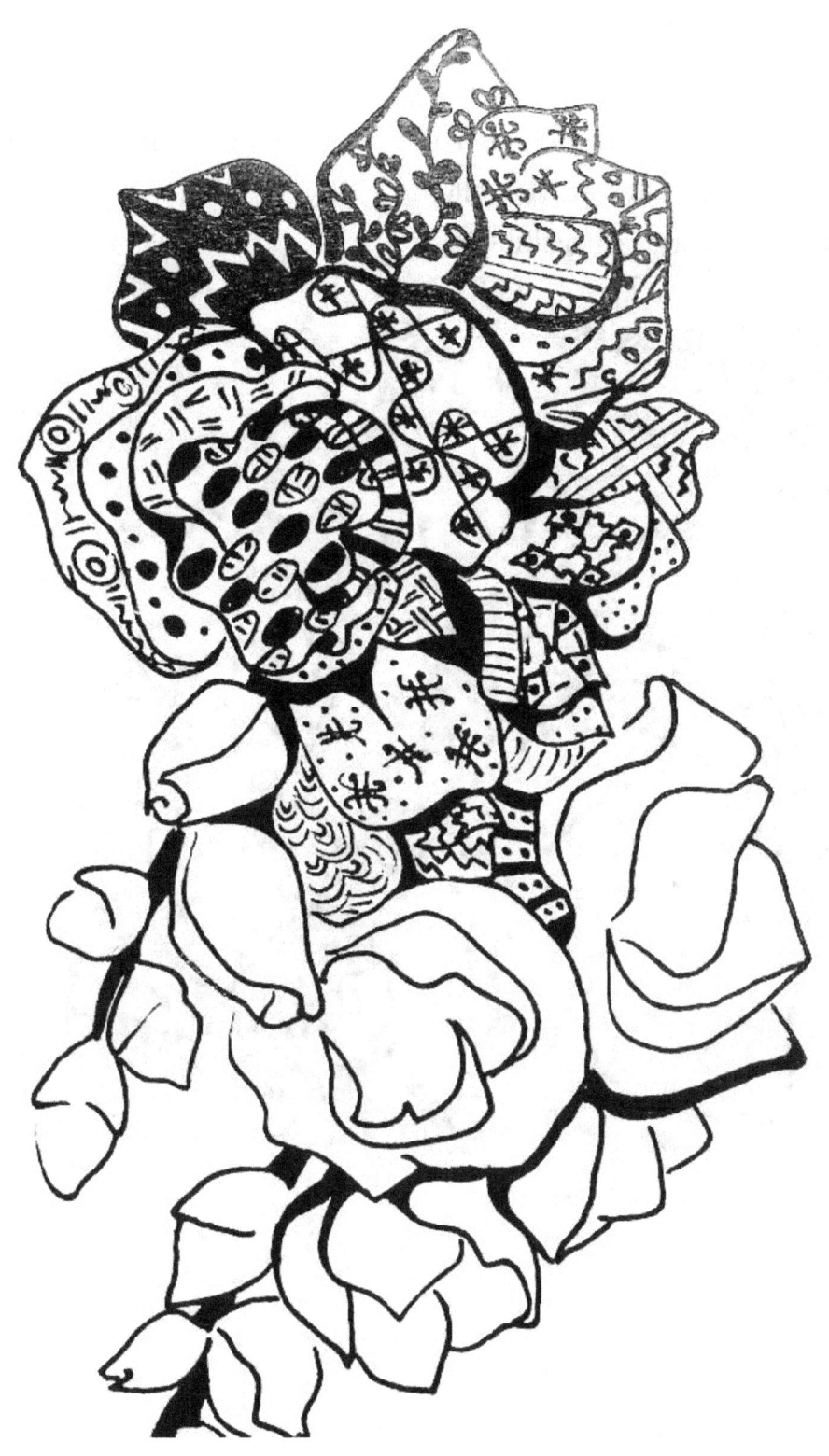

Step 6

Draw a few diamonds in the upper portion of flowers and surround them with circles. Draw a few arcs parallel to each other, a few negative bullets, and a small number of zigzag lines.

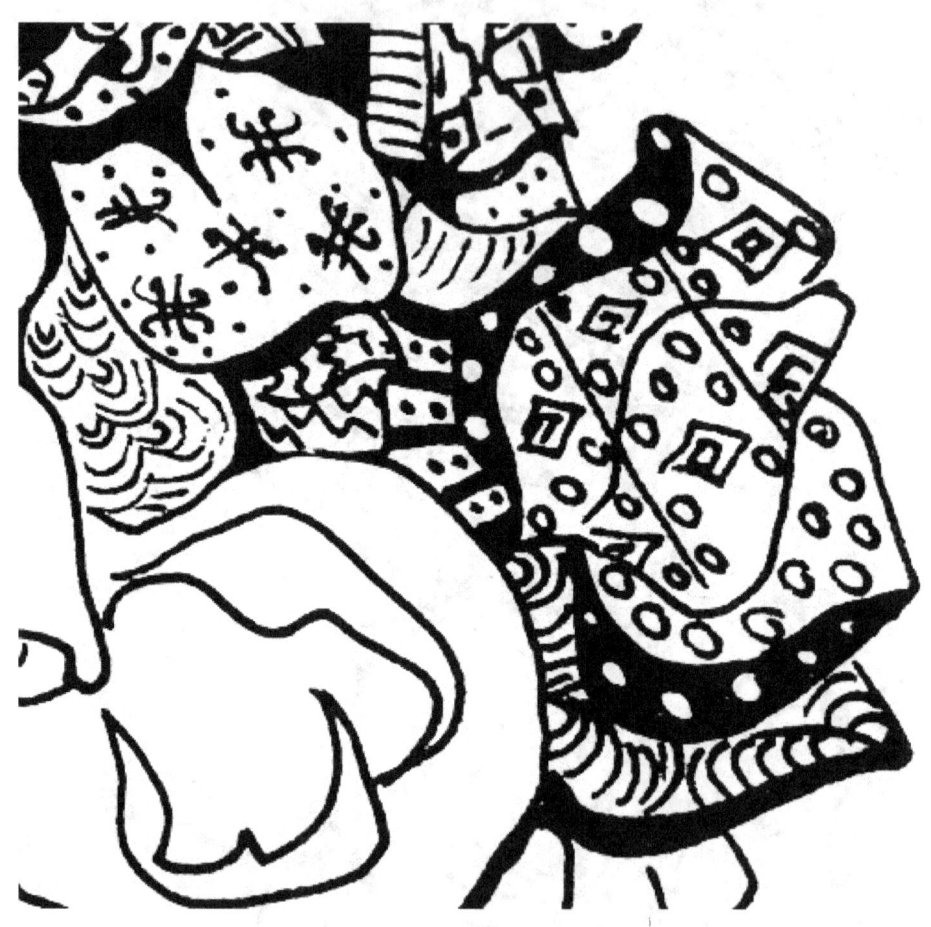

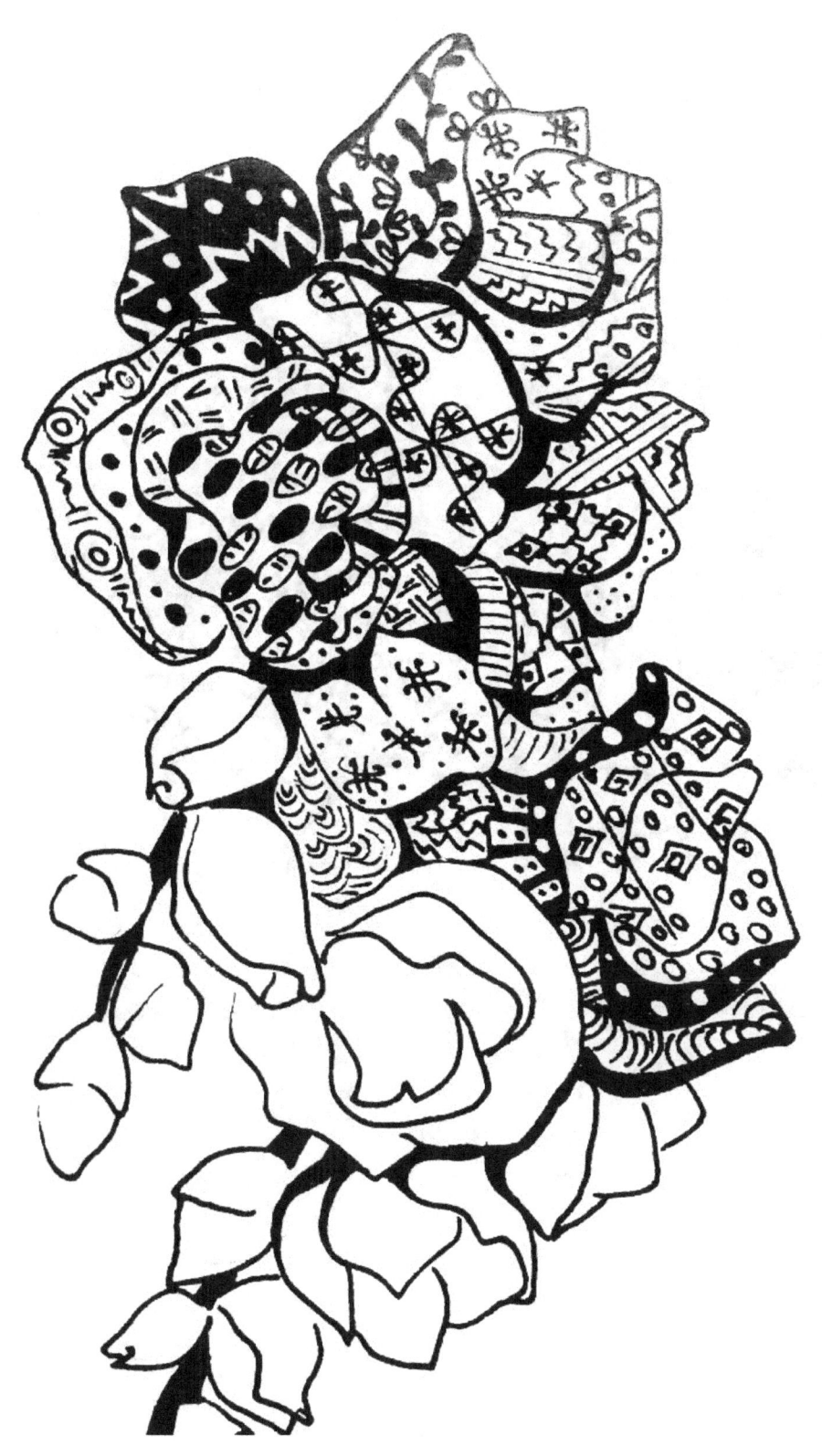

Step 7

Draw a few lines joined like that in a comb. Draw a few parallel and vertical lines.

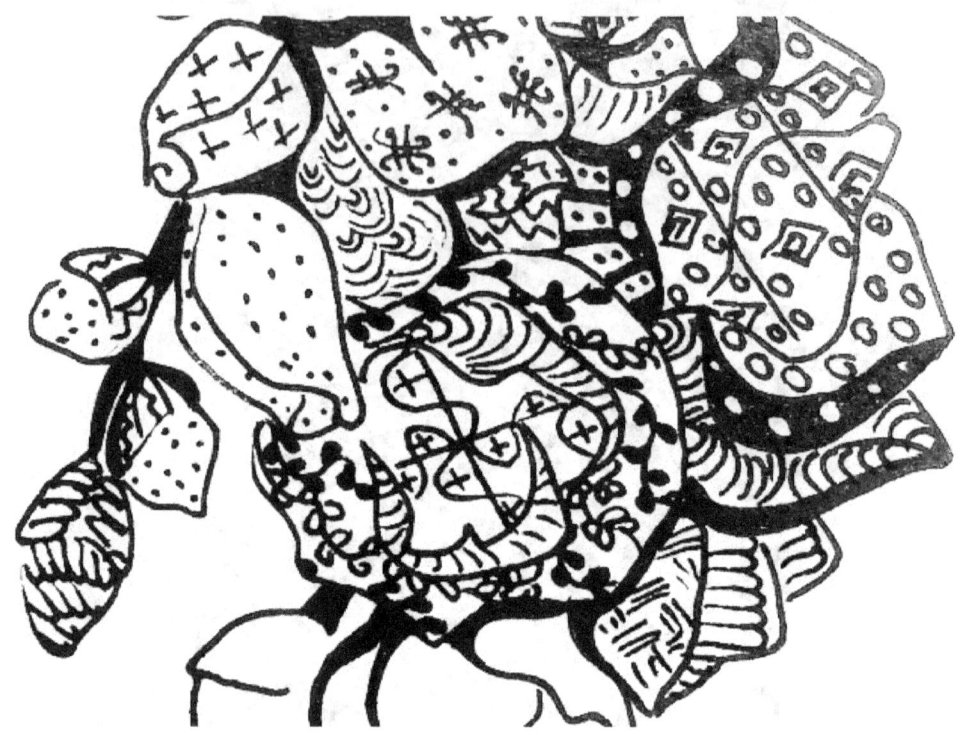

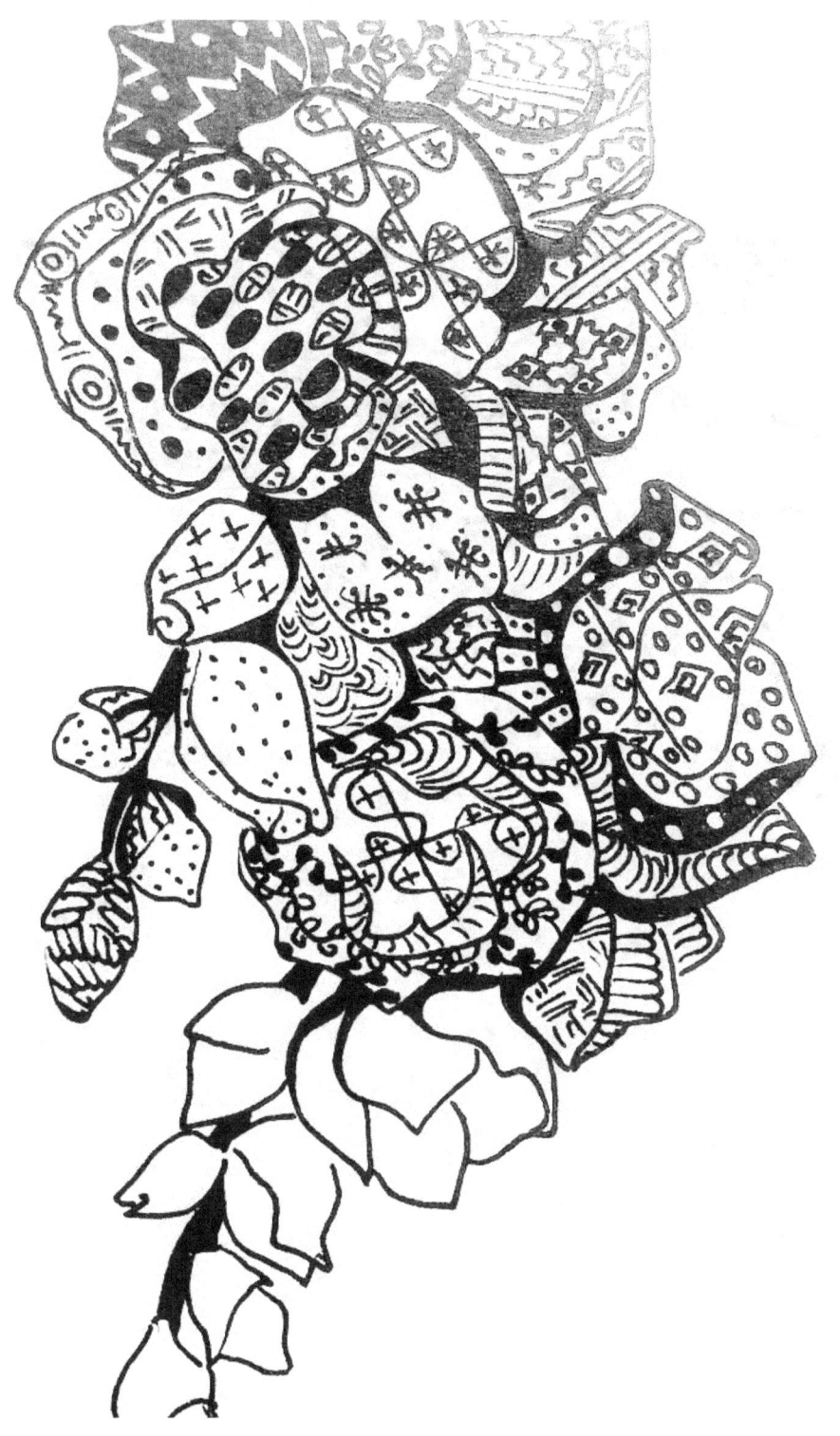

Step 8

In the lower section of the flowers, draw a few dots, '+' signs, and thick lines.

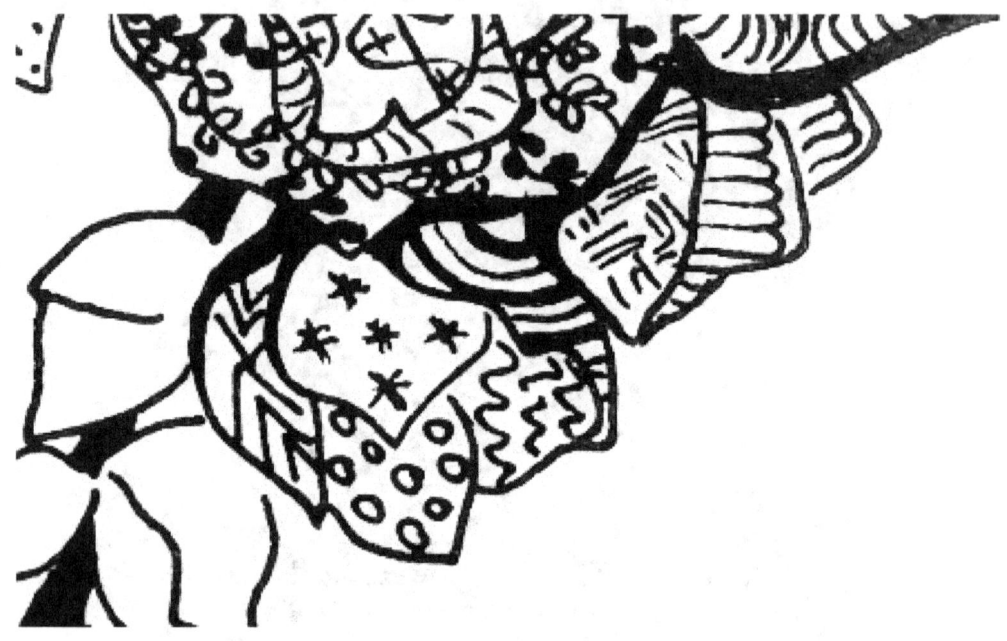

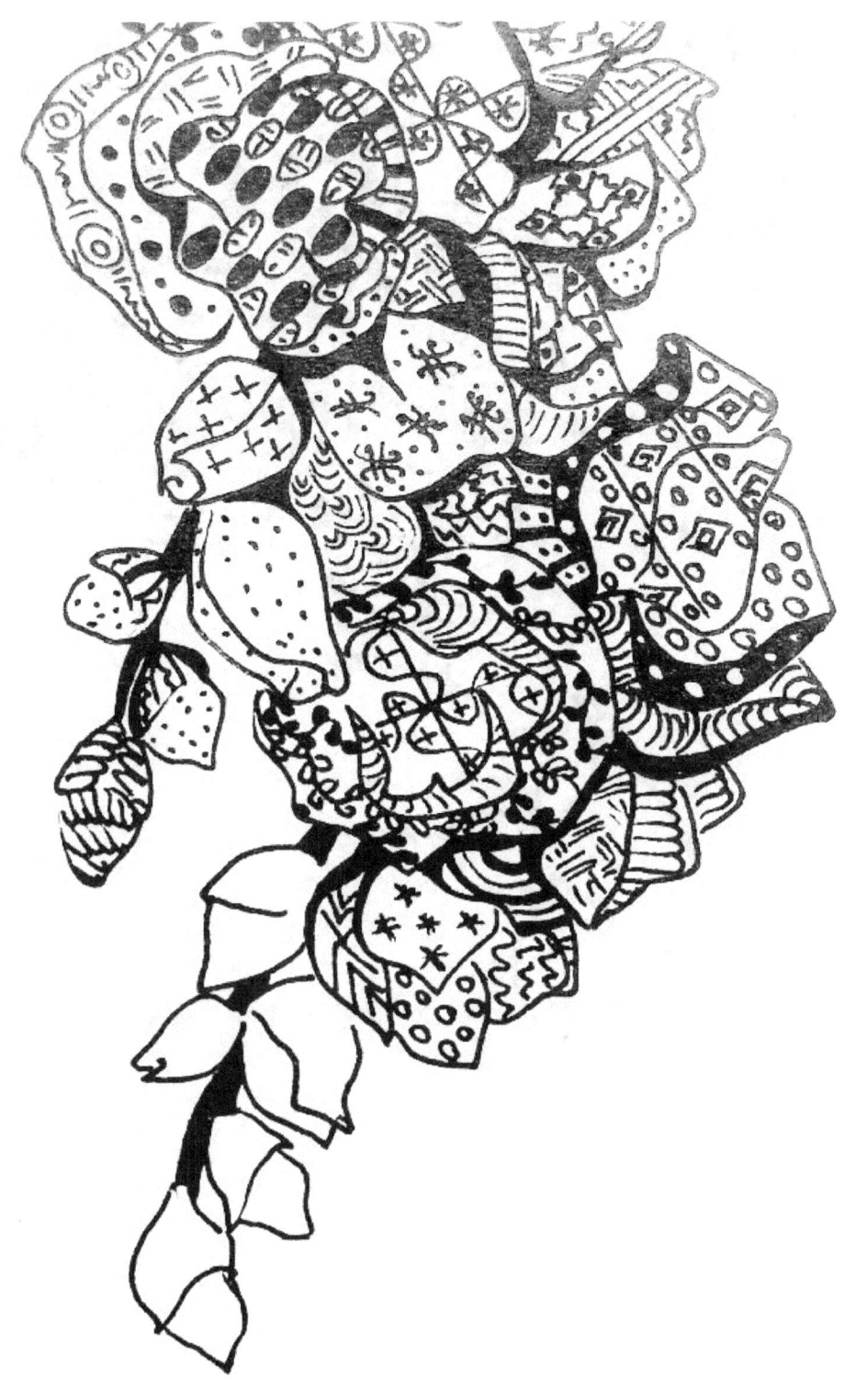

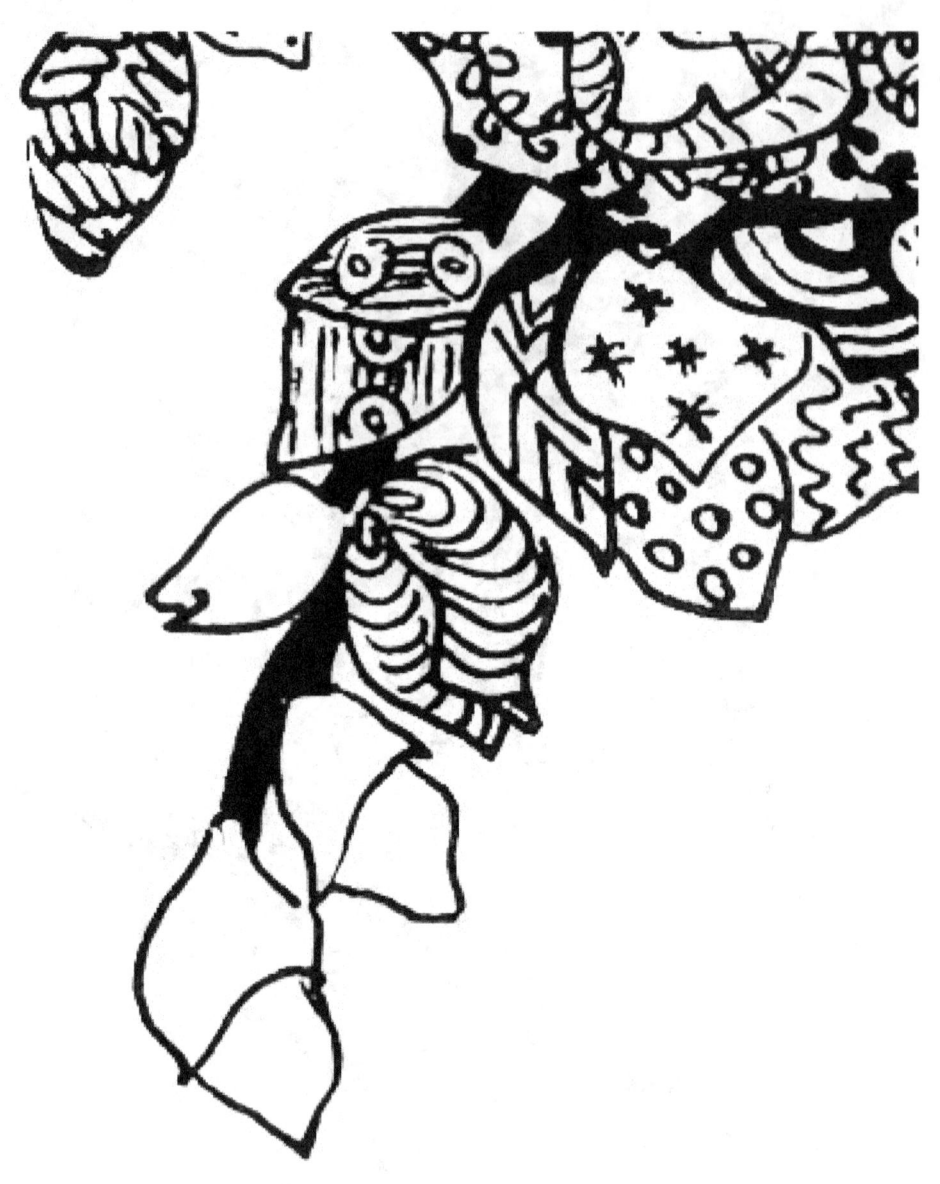

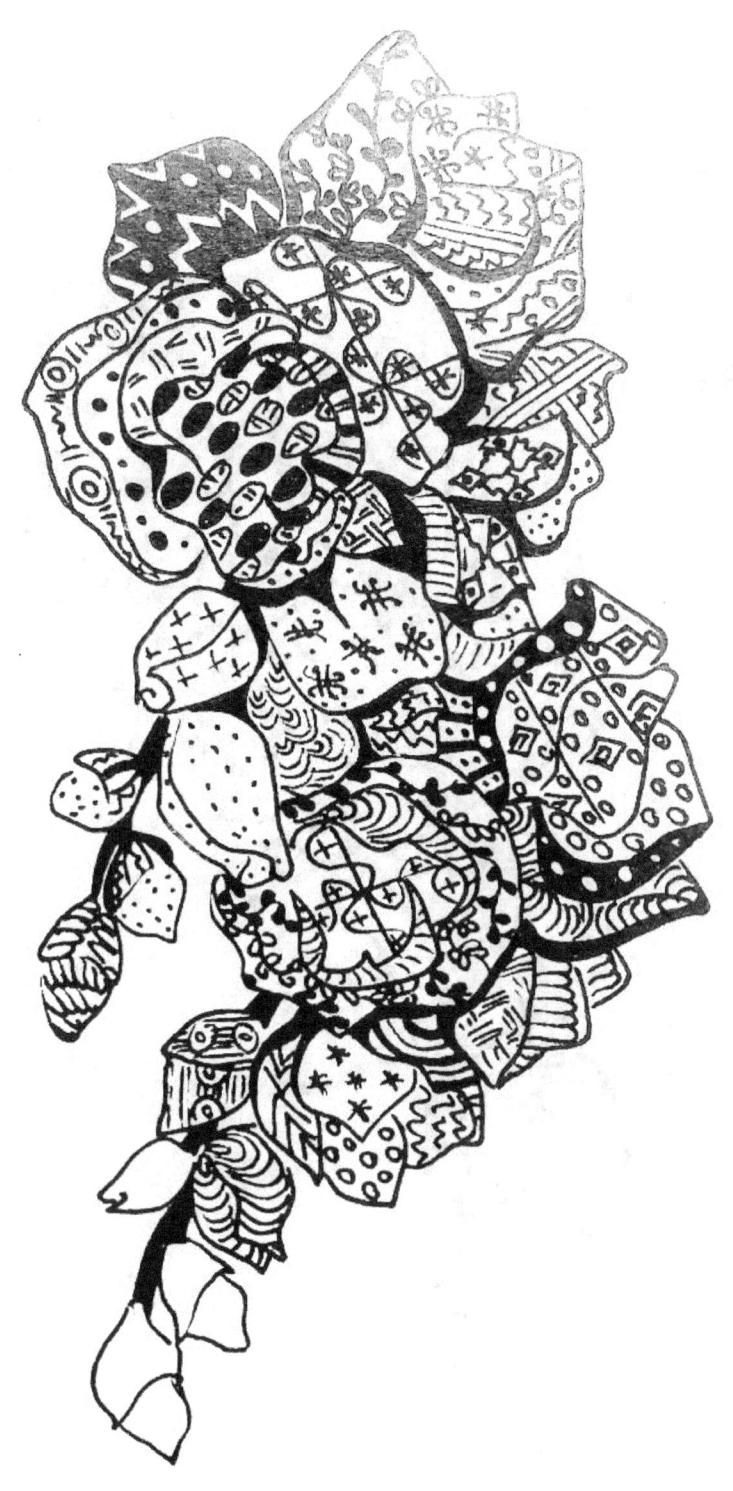

Step 9

In the right side of the flowers, draw a few scallops, flowers, thick lines, and any other pattern you want.

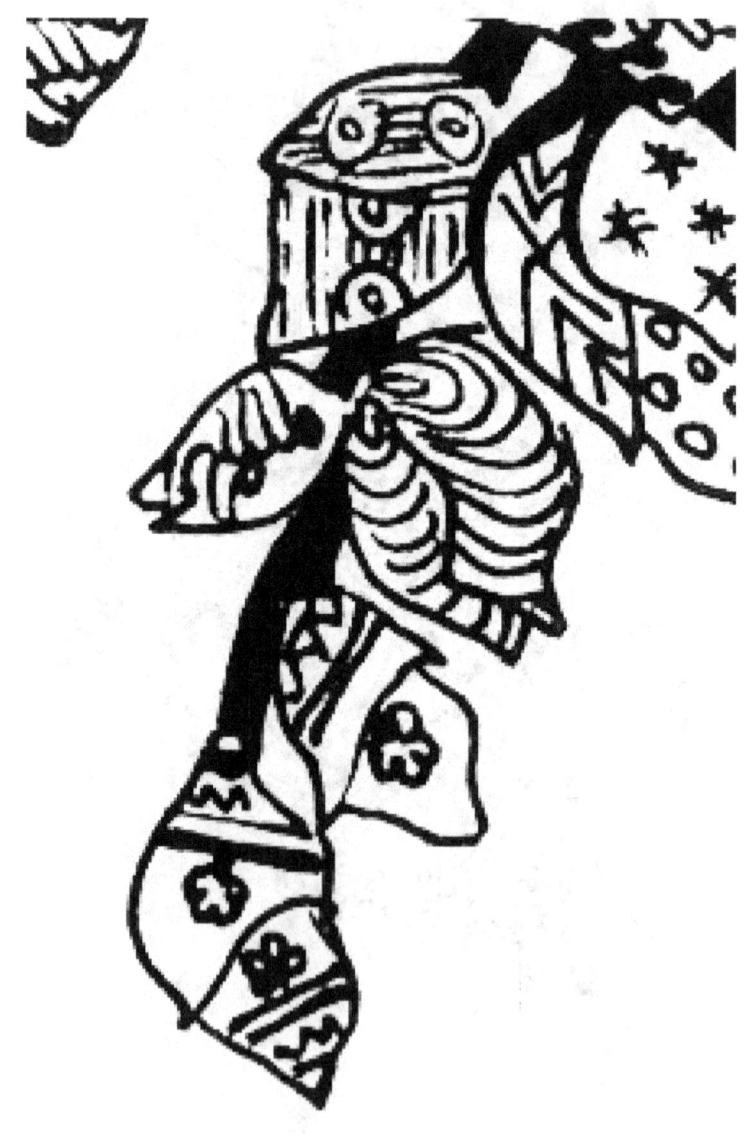

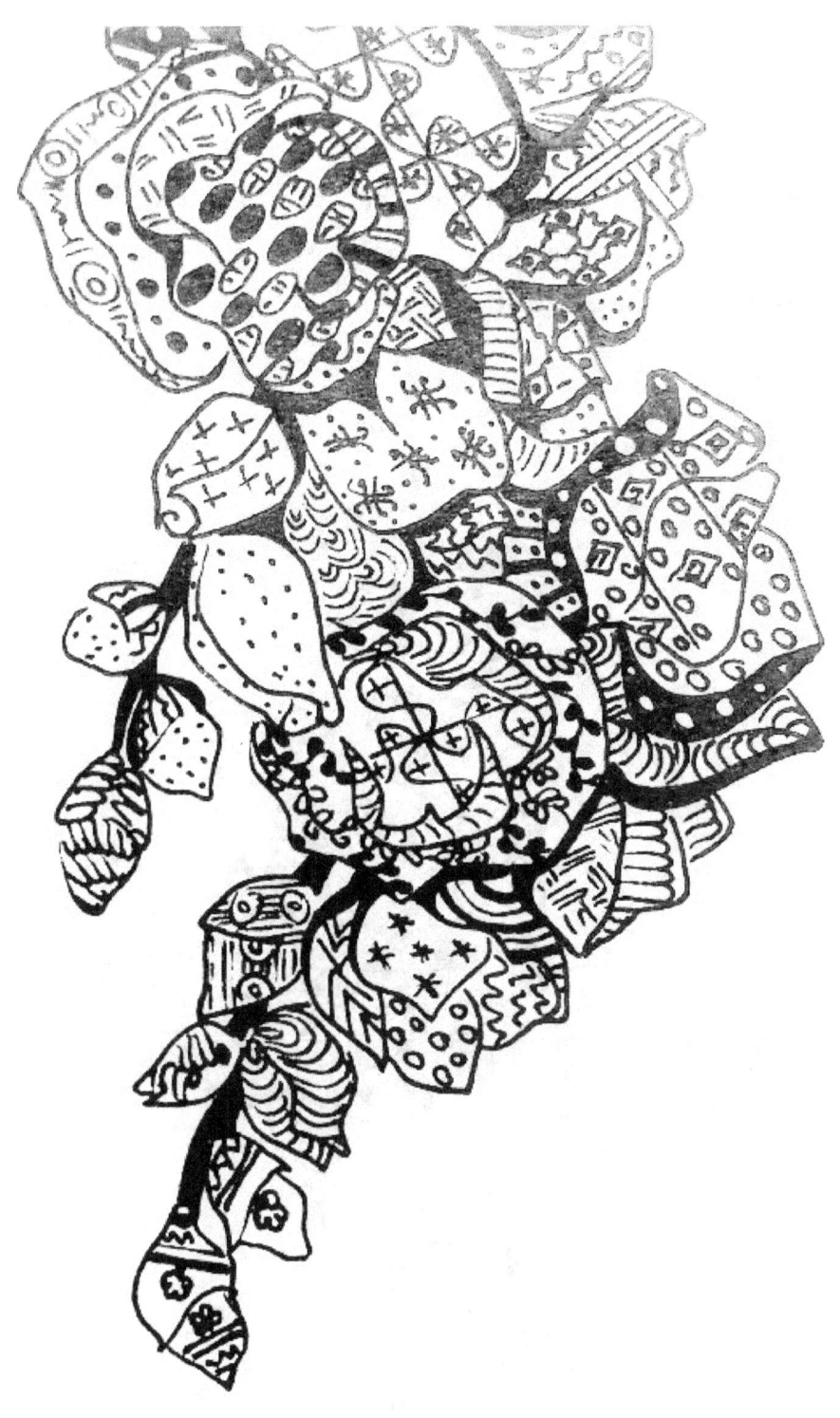

Step 10

Draw a few scribbles of horizontal lines on both sides of the flowers as shown in the picture. This is done when we draw a structure like that of flowers. Such lines on the sides of the flowers are used to bind the loose structure drawn in the illustration.

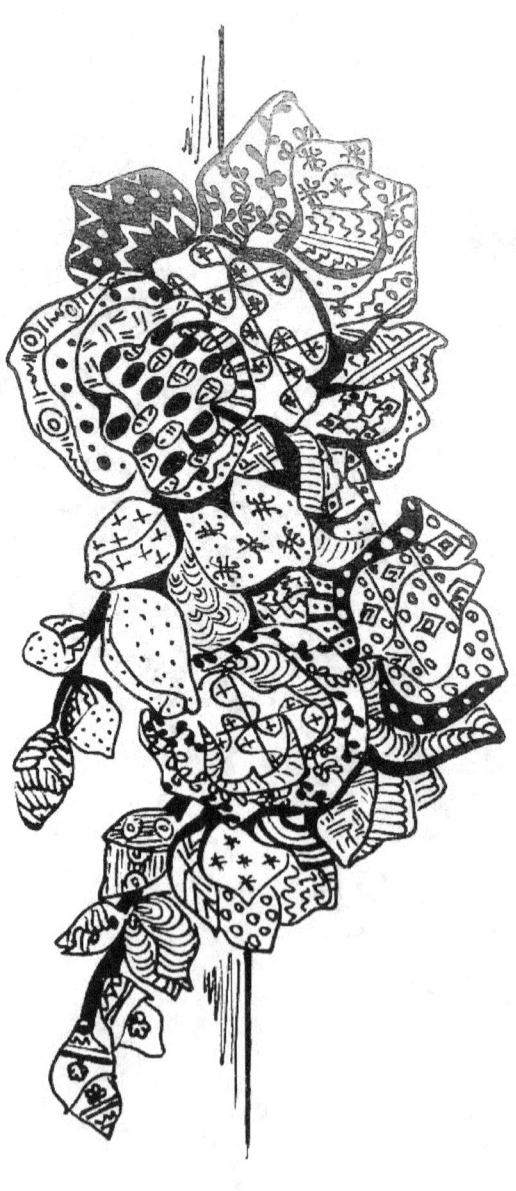

Drawing 4
Girl

Step 1

Draw the basic outline of a girl with its back towards the viewer and a slight side of the face is visible. The girl is wearing a hat.

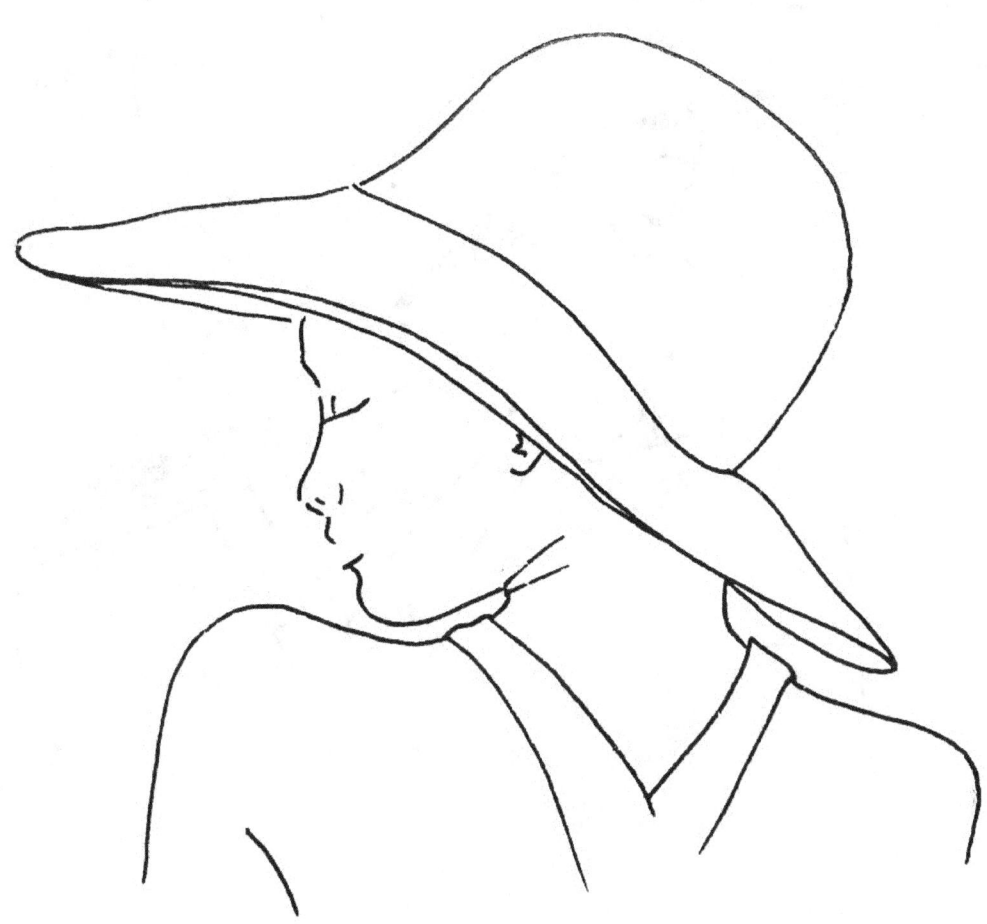

Step 2

Draw a string of dots on the face of the girl as shown in the picture.

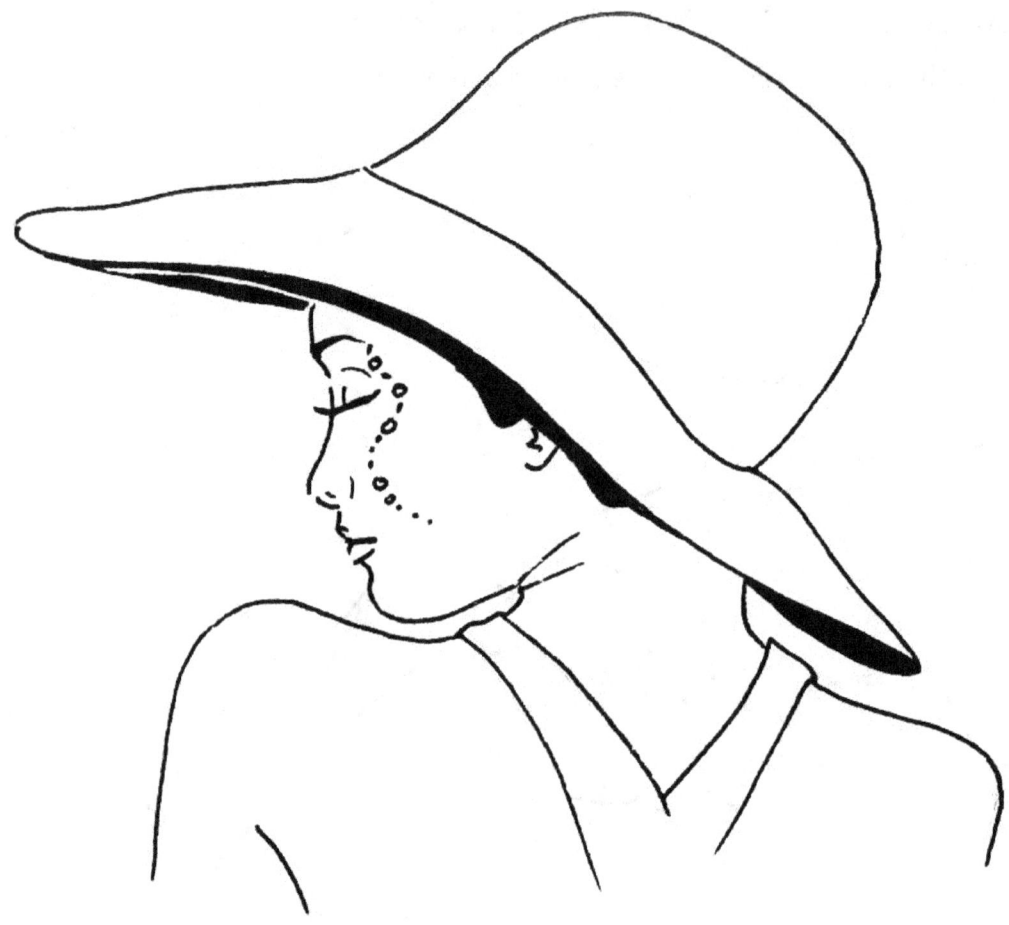

Step 3

Draw a diagonal line to divide the upper portion of the hat into two parts and then draw the galem pattern in one-half of the hat of the girl.

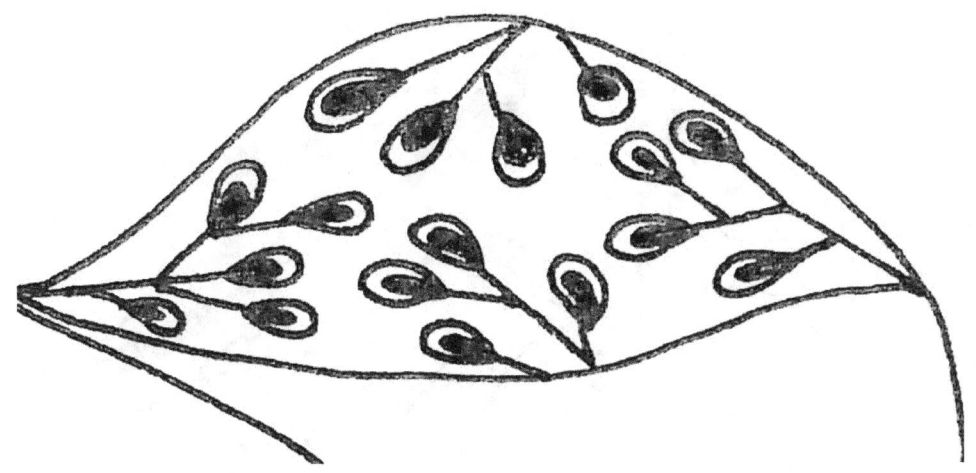

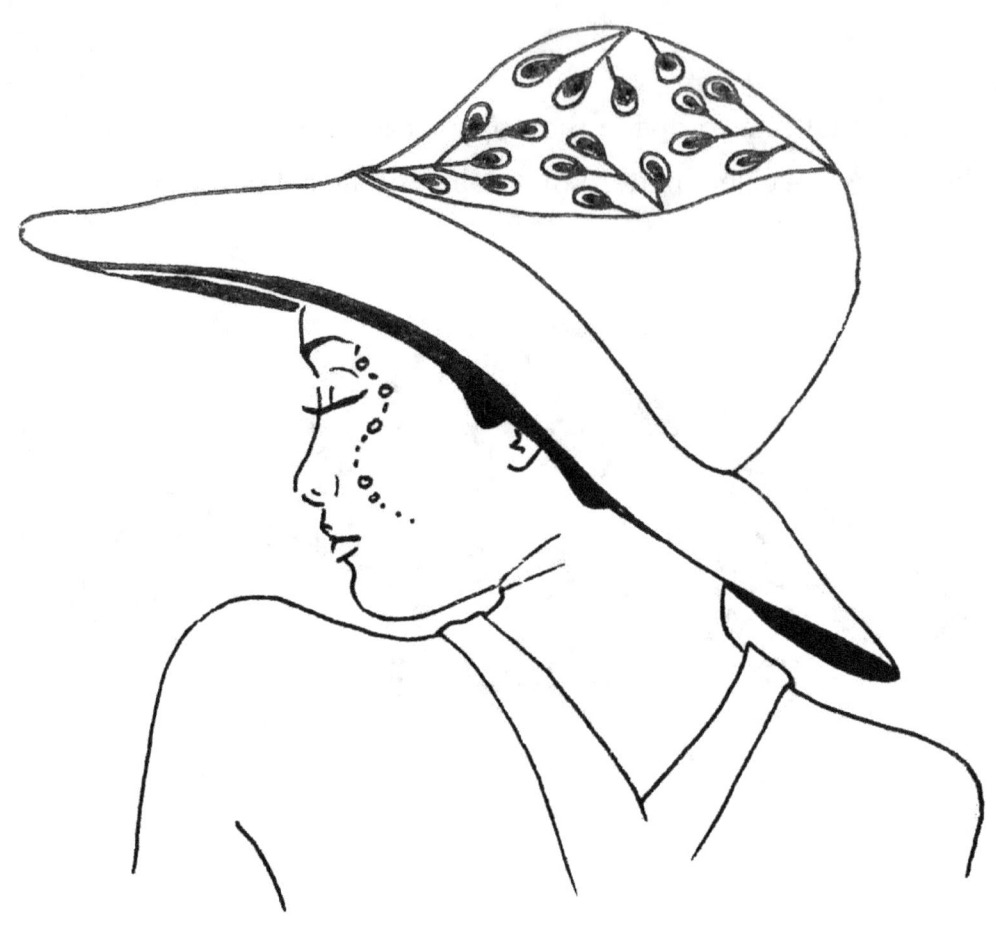

Step 4

In the other half of the hat, draw the flub pattern.

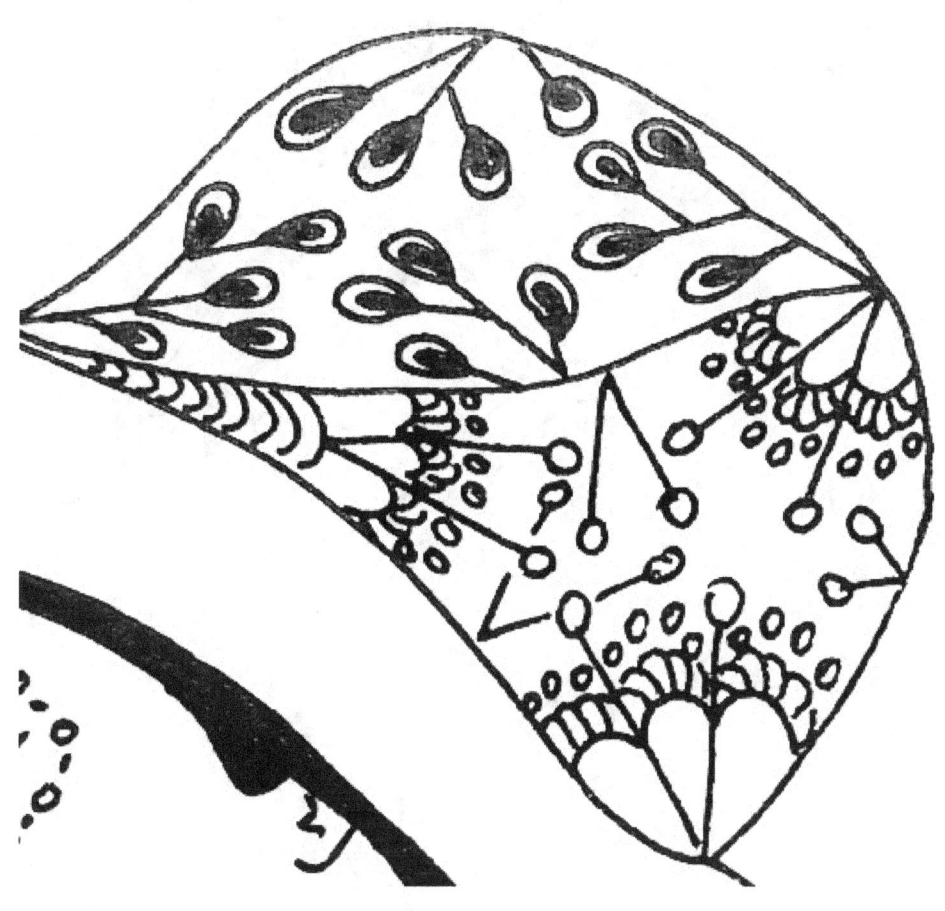

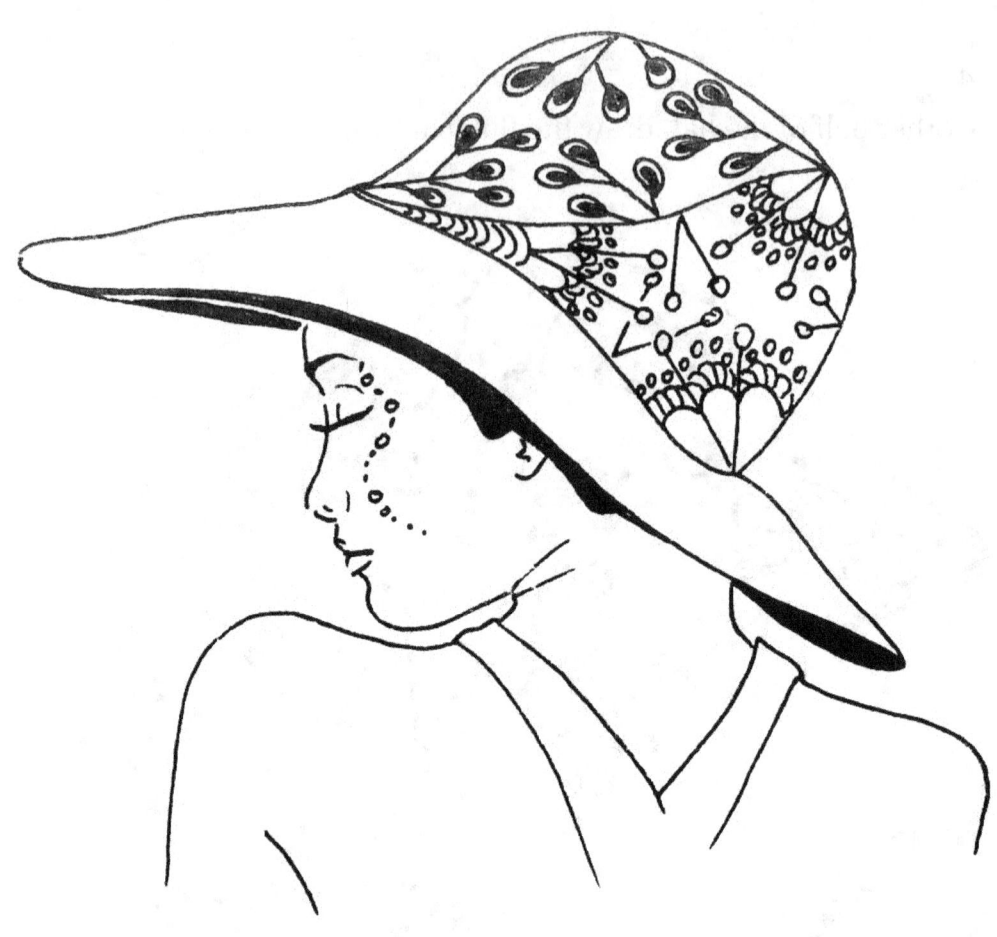

Step 5

In the base of the hat, draw the benif pattern in the left side. Draw the isry pattern in the middle portion accompanied by the scallops. Draw a few flowers in the right side of the hat and surround them with dots.

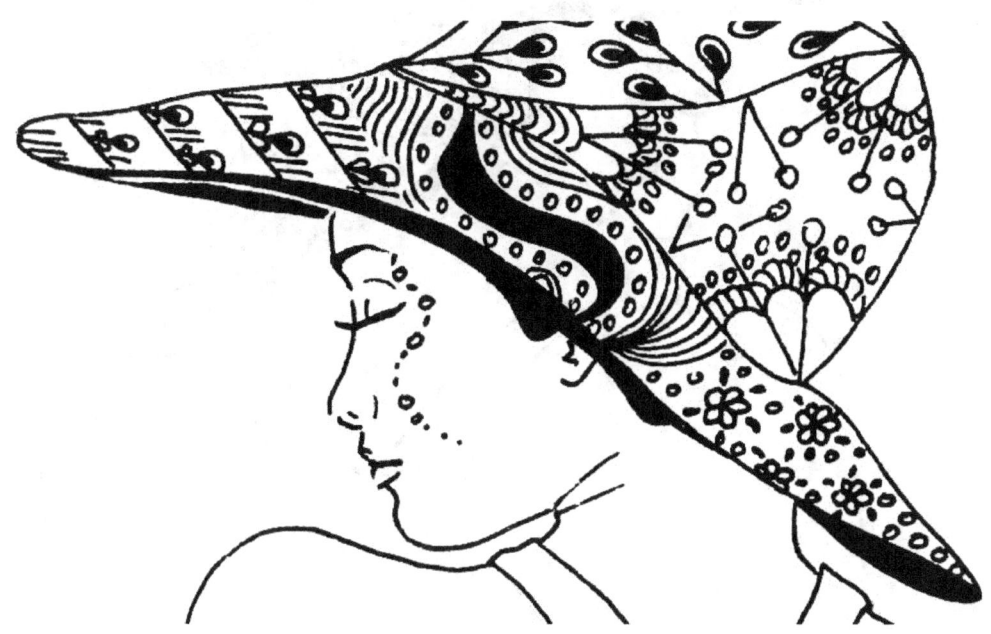

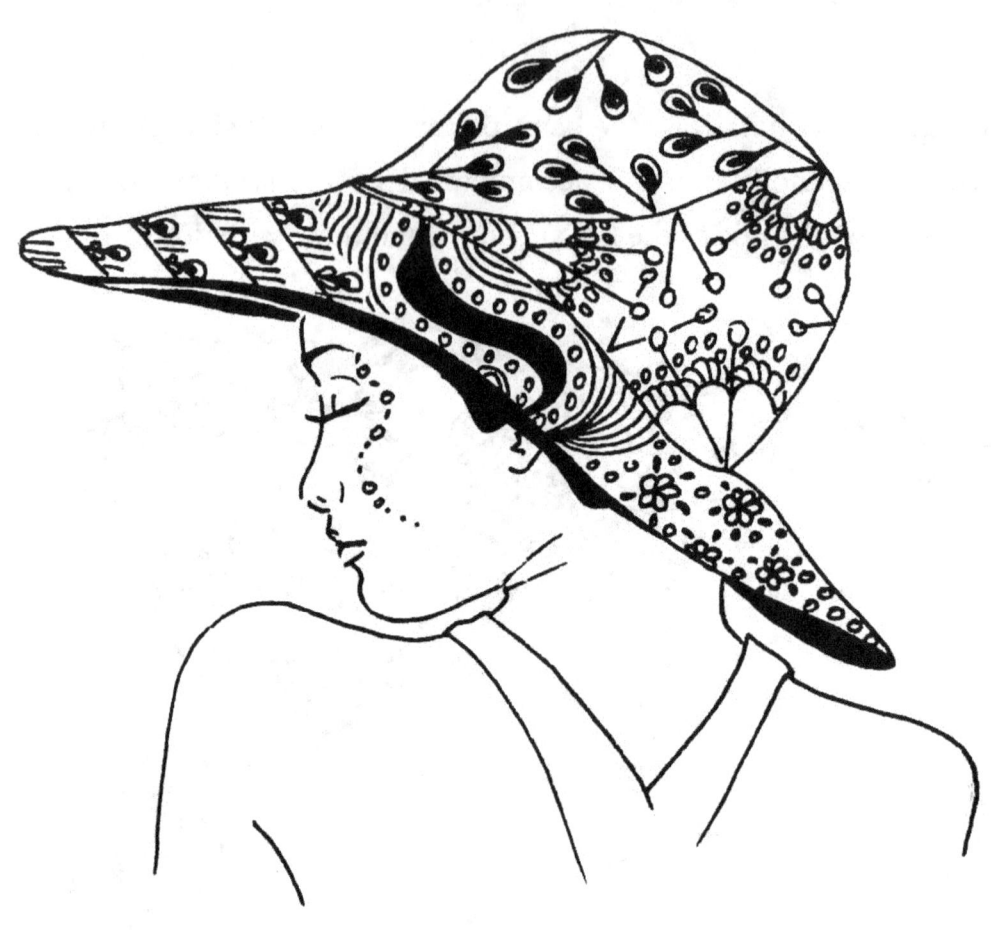

Step 6

Draw a few patterns such as circles, zigzag lines, thick stripes, swirls, horizontal lines, etc, in the strap of the girl's dress.

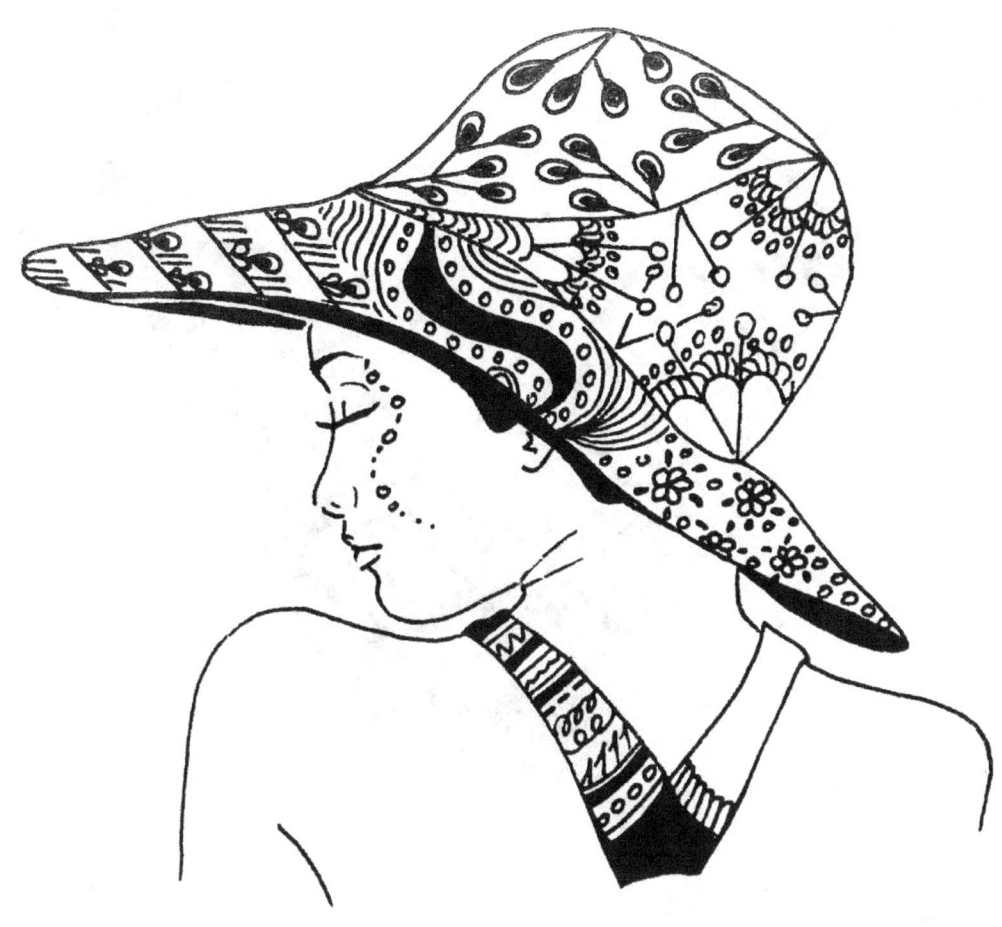

Step 7

Draw the similar patterns in the other strap of the dress.

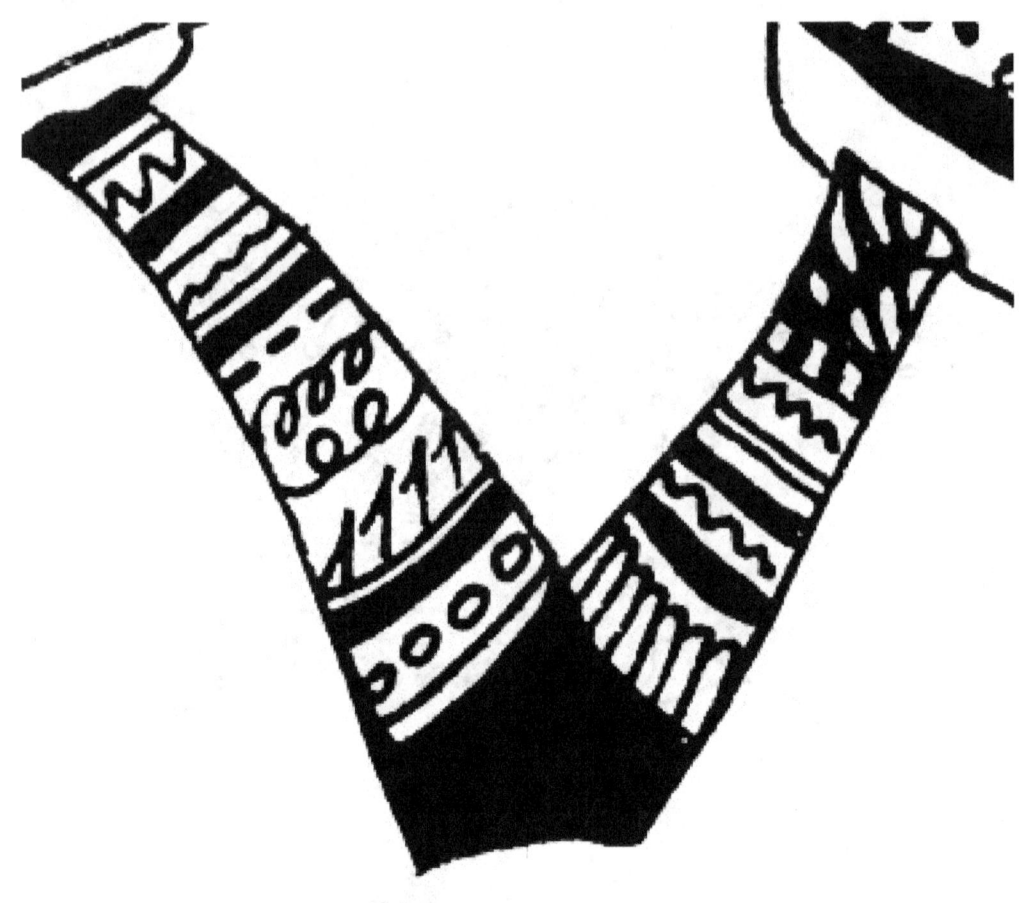

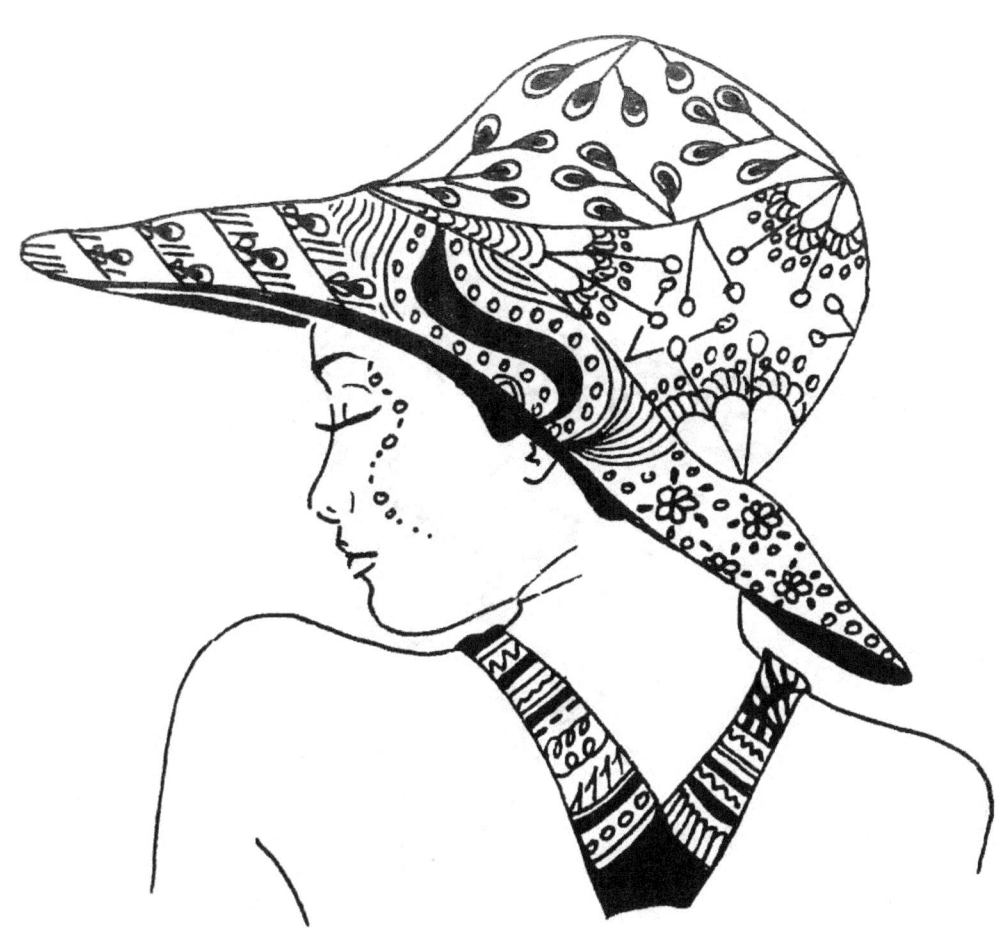

Step 8

Draw a few large arcs around the girl as shown in the picture.

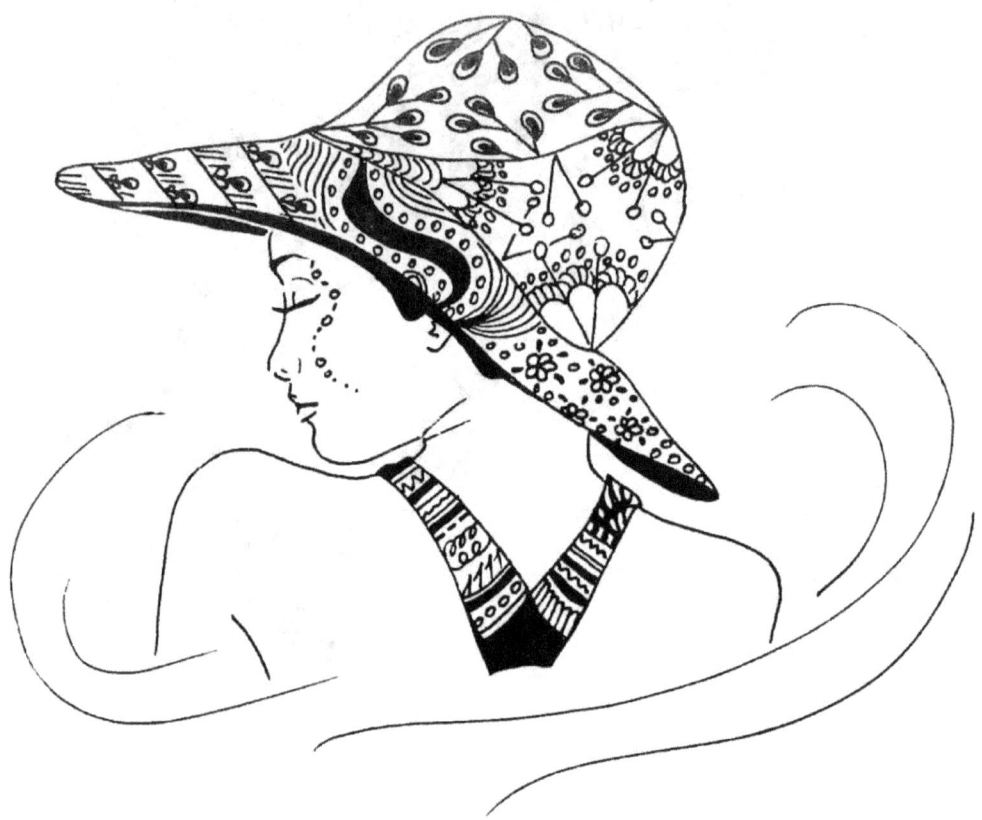

Step 9

Draw a blend of drops and paisley patterns on the tip of arcs as shown in the picture.

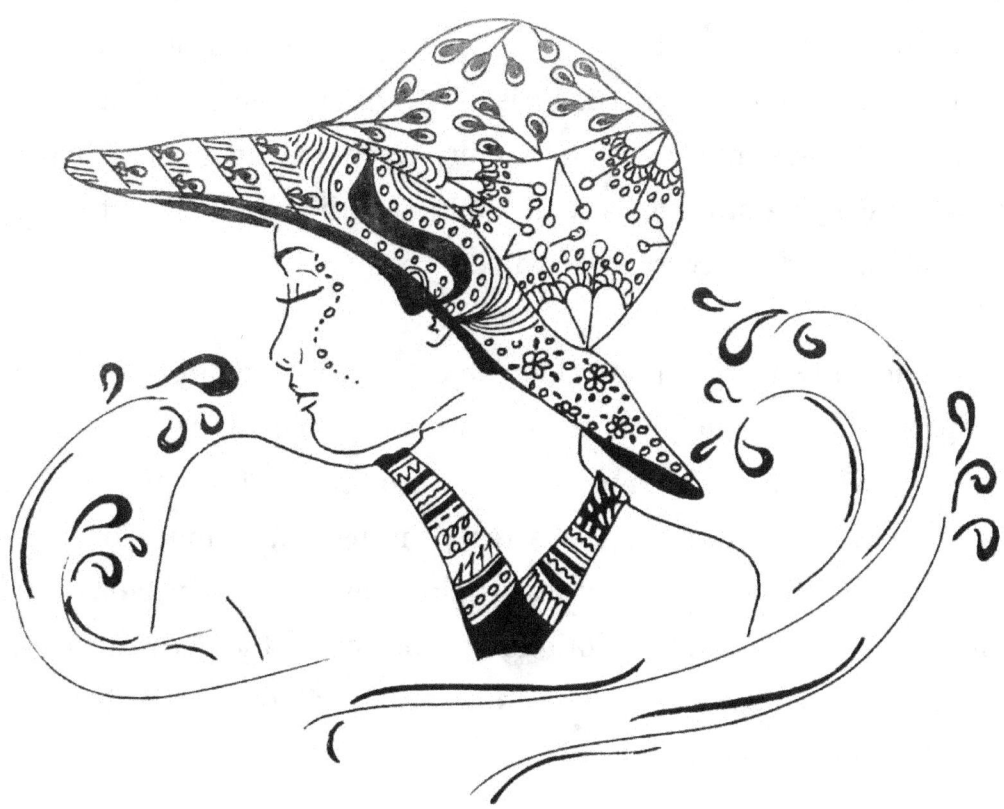

Conclusion

After reading and drawing patters of Zen Doodle from this book, it certainly feels better about the concept. It is important for an artist to create his/ her own drawings. One cannot progress as an individual artist or leave an impression on the world if one keeps copying the works of other artists. When the Renaissance age began, artists like Da Vinci emerged and became popular only because they were more interested in creating their own works, rather than copying other artists. In addition, it became crucial to make a few alterations to the process of drawing.

At that time, drawings became a new project; a new way of planning things on paper, with the help of a few sketches that were close to the brainstorming random words or impressions on paper. It became especially useful when the artist targeted to create a painting or a sculpture of a person because their sketches permitted free exploration of skin tones or muscles. For instance, the folds in the clothing of a person or the deconstruction of the facial expressions of a person were explored without any restriction on paper. This gave birth to original drawings of the artist.

The quick scribbles are followed by a formal string of study of the subject in consideration. This subject is later sculptured or painted accordingly with a full array of drawings. For instance, when you have to draw a cartoon strip, you draw only one scene after practicing them repeatedly. The same is the case with scribbles or Zen Doodle patterns. You might have to draw them one after another before you get a perfect design.

Although initially, drawings became famous as a part of planning for something important, now they have attained a completely different status. Presently, drawings are regarded as something like meditation. You can take up doodling if you have problems in your personal life. The drawing cannot solve your problems, but it can give you the strength to deal with the issues. If you get a chance to look at the drawings of legendry artists like Leonardo da Vinci, you will realize the genius that resided in them. Even the casual doodles of these artists are no less a masterpiece.

You can begin drawing according to your potential and enhance your skills with time. Do not forget to carry a notebook along with you wherever you go. You can utilize your free time when you have nothing to do to make doodles and create new designs.

Thank you!

Thank you for choosing our book, we hope you found it interesting and helpful.

If you liked the book, please give us a favor to write your review.

We would really appreciate this!

If you would like to have a bonus – **FREE BOOK**, please send the screenshot of your review to this e-mail: **lucy.artbooks@gmail.com** and we will send you a **FREE BOOK** in PDF as a **GIFT!****

Hope to see you in our future books and good luck in your drawing experience!

** in the e-mail subject please mention the name of the book you reviewed and the author.

www.ingramcontent.com/pod-product-compliance
Lightning Source LLC
Chambersburg PA
CBHW081153180526
45170CB00006B/2052